BIRDS, BEASTS AND ICE

AN ANTARCTIC ADVENTURE

Michael Anderson

Published by Dolman Scott in 2022

ISBN: 978-1-8384967-9-1
eBook: 978-1-8384967-1-5

Published by Dolman Scott
www.dolmanscott.com

DEDICATION ·

To my beautiful wife Jane for your love and support and for all that you have taught me. Your light shines brightly and brings joy, smiles and laughter to all who meet you.

To my sister and great friend Caroline, healer and artist extraordinaire.

Finally, to Antarctica for just being there and to the remarkable wildlife that inhabits its environs.

'If Antarctica were music, it would be Mozart. Art, and it would be Michelangelo. Literature, and it would be Shakespeare. And yet it is something even greater; the only place on earth that is still as it should be. May we never tame it.'

Andrew Denton (Australian Television Producer).

CONTENTS

INTRODUCTION

Few of us can afford to travel to Antarctica. Cruise prices per person, including flights etc start at US $9,000 to the Antarctic Peninsula and increase to a starting price of US$25,000 for tours to more remote areas. I was fortunate to spend six months in Antarctica as a volunteer biologist working with Adélie penguins; my voyages, accommodation, food and clothing were all provided for me. This is an account of my time there. In writing this book, my aim is that others, who might never be able to journey there, can see it through my eyes. I also hope to raise awareness of this special place and its wildlife and the threats they now face.

Antarctica is a land like no other, a place of soaring ice cliffs, flowing glaciers, icebergs the size of towns, unique wildlife and mountain ranges that emerge through blue ice laid down hundreds of thousands, perhaps millions of years ago.

Voyage with me across the world's wildest ocean and into a frozen sea, the ship breaking ice for thousands of kilometres towards Mawson station, East Antarctica. From the ship, a helicopter takes you the last 400 kilometres to the research base which is perched on the edge of the polar icecap. Experience life in a field camp adjacent to an Adélie penguin rookery. Ride on quad bikes over the ice super-highway to Auster emperor penguin rookery and sit quietly while looking directly into the eyes of the world's tallest penguin.

Ski over the fast ice to towering icebergs and sit with Weddell seals and their beautiful velvety pups while listening to the males singing beneath the ice. Walk on the icecap; climb Antarctic mountains and experience howling blizzards, the like of which Scott and his party endured over a hundred years ago.

This is your chance to go where few people ever tread without leaving home. I hope that you will voyage with me to the bottom of the world, to the highest, driest, coldest continent on earth.

CHAPTER 1:

VOYAGE TO ANTARCTICA

The gangplank was raised, massive ropes cast off fore and aft and a long blast on the ship's horn signalled departure. A lattice of coloured paper streamers stretched from the hands of those on board to loved ones on the wharf. The brass band played jolly tunes, the mood both happy and sad. The *RSV Aurora Australis* affectionately known as the Big Orange Ship or Orange Roughy, was underway, the streamers stretching and then breaking; paper connections severed but lasting bonds intact.

Figure 1: RSV Aurora Australis, 95-metres long and 6,574 gross tonnes. The icebreaker was launched in 1989. The open flying bridge is directly above the enclosed (windowed) bridge. Credit: Bahnfrend on Wikimedia Commons.

The Australian research and resupply vessel steamed down the Derwent Estuary into Storm Bay, enjoying final views of Hobart and Kununyi (Mount Wellington), as our six-week 5,545-kilometre journey to Mawson Station, Antarctica commenced. My previous ocean-going experience amounted to ferry rides, maximum three hours in duration. This was a vastly different proposition, a journey across the world's wildest ocean from the roaring forties, through the furious fifties, the screaming sixties and beyond. Ten days of open ocean followed by weeks in the pack-ice. Antarctica: the world's highest, driest and coldest continent has a land mass of 14.2 million square kilometres, with up to 20 million square kilometres of sea ice by springtime. This was the third week of September; it was warming up in Tasmania but as we travelled south, temperatures would fall rapidly.

The Australian Antarctic Division (AAD) owns and maintains three scientific research stations on the Antarctic continent: Casey, Davis and Mawson. The bases are manned by personnel (known as expeditioners) of the Australian National Antarctic Research Expeditions (ANARE). Each station is resupplied annually, and the personnel are also usually changed at that time. Expeditioners, mostly trades people, are deployed for 12 months, and are known as winterers while others, mainly scientific staff, are there for six months and are known as summerers.

On this trip it was the turn of Davis station to be resupplied as the ocean nearby is often ice free much earlier in the spring than the other two. But we were to call in or get as close as possible - pack-ice allowing- to Casey and Mawson too. This would undoubtedly involve the use of helicopters of which there were two on board.

The three Australian stations are widely separated, the greatest distance being 1,400 kilometres between Casey and Davis. From there it was a further 637 kilometres to Mawson although we would be unlikely to get closer than 100 kilometres due to extensive sea ice. First, we had to cross around 3,000 kilometres of ocean.

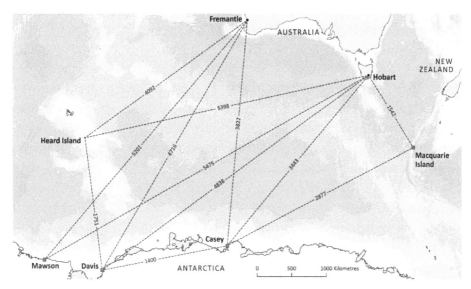

Figure 2: Direct distances between Fremantle, Western Australia and Hobart, Tasmania to Australia's three Antarctic and one sub-Antarctic stations. Heard Island is shown but does not have a continuously manned field station. Credit: Australian Antarctic Division

Sites on which to build stations in Antarctica are scarce as only about 0.2% of the continent is ice free and therefore suitable for doing so. The main ice-free areas are the Antarctic peninsula and the coast of Queen Maud Land which lies far to the west of the peninsula. Between the two areas there are many stations belonging to dozens of nations. These stations, especially those on the peninsula, are far less costly to supply being close to the port of Ushuaia in southern Argentina. This port also supports the main Antarctic tourist trade, with tens of thousands paying big bucks to visit the peninsula every Austral summer.

East Antarctica, where Mawson station is situated, is a more remote area of the continent with few ice-free sites, hence research stations are more scattered and generally further apart than on the Antarctic Peninsula. It also means that very few tourist vessels venture anywhere near Mawson station, the closest usually being to Sir Douglas Mawson's old hut at Cape Denison, Commonwealth Bay, 1,400 kilometres east of Casey station. Mawson's hut is over 3,400 kilometres from Mawson station but the two often get confused.

Together with my boss or supervisor, a group of three geologists, two Bureau of Meteorology weather observers and several other personnel, I was headed to Mawson for spring and summer. My role was as a volunteer biologist assisting the paid researcher (or supervisor) on a long-term study of Adélie penguins. The two of us would be stationed at a field camp on Béchervaise Island (known as Bech) about four kilometres from the main station. Every week or two, weather and fast ice allowing, we would travel to the station for hot showers and to do laundry etc, often staying for one or two nights.

The food on board the Orange Roughy was said to be excellent and this, combined with not wanting to miss a minute of the voyage, persuaded me to take seasickness pills. They induced a not unpleasant dreamy effect and while others that did not take them were often cabin-bound I was able to roam the ship and to attend mealtimes. I shared a cabin with two other blokes, making it crowded when we were all there but that was only at bedtime, which even then varied between us. Our external cabin had a porthole. I'm not claustrophobic but having a tiny window onto the world helped me breath better. The cabin on D deck was comfy and had an en-suite. In big seas, standing and showering was often a challenge while peeing was of necessity a seated experience. Ocean going ships are designed to prevent accident and injury, a high lip on the shower tray avoids a flooded cabin and grab rails help you remain upright, while the bunks have high sides. Trying to sleep while the ship rocks and rolls in stormy seas was a real challenge. On such occasions I used all of my clothes and extra pillows to wedge myself in and reduce sideways and longitudinal movement. I knew of one expeditioner who attached large amounts of Velcro to his sleeping bag and to the cabin walls to prevent movement but that seemed excessive.

The first few days saw relatively calm seas with swells of two to three meters. Once past Tasmania's southern outliers: Pedra Branca and Eddystone Rocks, there is nothing but a vast open ocean. Coastal seabirds such as silver gulls and pacific gulls were soon replaced by the denizens of the wind: prions, petrels and shearwaters and their massive cousins the albatrosses. At this stage they were mainly shy albatrosses, their breeding islands being relatively close to Tasmania.

As promised, the food onboard was great, meals seeming to follow one another on a constantly moving conveyor belt: breakfast, lunch and dinner, thanks to the dedicated kitchen staff. The ice strengthened vessel has five inside decks plus the engine room: decks A down to E with the bridge designated A, officer and crew quarters are on decks B and C below it. Passenger cabins and a movie theatre are on D-deck, E-deck has the kitchen and mess, lounge and library.

Also, on E-deck are science and wet labs with a trawl deck at the stern. C-deck provides access to external walkways and to the bows and the stern via heavy sea doors that are kept closed in big seas. A large helicopter hangar that housed two Sikorsky S76 choppers lay at the rear of C-deck. Beyond that, near the stern, is a large open helideck, railed to prevent accidents, and with a large painted yellow circle on a green background with the letter H within. Looking out from the rear railings at sea, the churning wake stretched far astern.

Above the bridge, which has extending wings either side, is an open flying bridge or monkey bridge. Up there past enormous kitchen vents, the ships mast and gantry rise high above with constantly rotating radar and a satellite communications dome. Forward of the mast is the open area of the flying bridge, its wings matching those of the bridge below. Strapped to the railings on the starboard side, is a small weather station: a louvred wooden box painted bright white containing mercury thermometers used as a backup and comparison of the ship's electronic sensors. Weather observations were conducted every three hours; so being a night owl I volunteered for the 9 pm and midnight slots.

Only three days into the voyage and I was already in a routine: I made it just in time for breakfast which is a delicious buffet: muesli then bacon, eggs and toast, washed down with English breakfast tea. I had a couple of hours out on deck watching albatrosses and other smaller seabirds and then it was time for lunch followed by another two hours on deck.

It was surprisingly quiet outside, many expeditioners remaining inside for the entire voyage, venturing out only for compulsory emergency drills held every Saturday morning. That was fine by me. I love solitude and most of the folk that were out there loved it too and enjoyed a chat about the bird life.

A three-course dinner came next. Mealtimes, especially dinner, were a real social occasion on the ship. In calm seas the large double-sided mess hummed with conversation, seeming to roll in waves like the ocean with the clank of pans, the clink of crockery and the raised voices of busy kitchen staff. There was great camaraderie on board: the ethos being that we were all in this together, old hands and new. With the mess full, the AAD voyage leader took the opportunity to announce housekeeping reminders and updates or, as we moved closer to the ice, he explained plans for marine science.

With a full belly, I rested and read in the lounge. Outside the sky darkened, the thrum of the engines now so familiar. Soon it was time for the nine o'clock weather observation and I headed to the bridge to log-on to the computer. Then kitted up I exited the bridge out into wind and rain, sometimes hail. I climbed metal stairways to the top of the ship. It was easy in calm seas, far more difficult as she rolled in a six-metre swell. To forge its way through ice the *Aurora Australis's* design concedes some stability. The result is that in rough seas she rolls like an exceptionally large pig!

On the flying bridge in 10-metre seas, it was incredibly exciting: the ships bow burying itself in the next massive swell, the resulting maelstrom clawing its way up over the bridge where the wipers attempted to clear the windscreens. The spume where I stood was like an old-time movie set, ten blokes with buckets, the making of vaudeville slapstick had it not been so real. Spitting sea water, I was hanging onto the starboard railing, as the ship rolled, looking down a 40-degree slope to the port rail. Had I let go, it would all be over in seconds as I hurtled down that frightening slope, tumbled over the railing and fell into ice-cold sea, outcome: certain death. I knew it was crazy to be up there. It's not that I'm an adrenalin junky, more that I'm in love with the wild and the elements; the thrill of being lashed by wind, sea, rain, hail and snow. I was riding the edge of sensibility knowing that a warm cabin awaited me.

After the weather observation I cast off my wet gear and headed down to the mess for a hot cuppa and some cake. There was always lots of food on offer in the evenings: dinner leftovers in the glass doored display case, dessert by its side, trays of cakes over by the hot drinks area. Some folks left the ship twice as heavy as when they boarded but that was not for me. There was a small gym in the bowels of the ship where we could exercise, although understandably the crew had priority. I hit the stationary bike and the rowing machine, but my main workout was climbing and descending internal and external stairways, from mess to bridge, stern to bows, always going somewhere: a better view here, another vantage point there. It was all part of my days and my nights, and we hadn't even reached the ice yet.

Figure 3: The Big Orange Ship rolling in rough seas in the Southern Ocean with wind driven sleet and snow gathering at the bows. Credit: © Graeme Snow / Alamy Stock Photo.

An hour after dinner, a cup of hot tea in my hand, I entered the movie theatre. Taking a minute for my eyes to adjust to the dark, I found a comfy seat. Movies go almost 24/7 on board and it was ships policy for someone to choose a movie each evening based on a rota system. Videos were rolled at 7.30 pm, the title posted on the mess white board. For me it was just a bit of time out, for others it was almost their entire shipboard life. I'd watch a while, perhaps even until the end credits if it was a good movie. Then it was time for another cup of tea before the nine o' clock weather observation.

Once I became proficient at identifying the different types of clouds and discerning the height and direction of sea and swell from 12-metres up on the bridge, weather observations only took 10-minutes. That left plenty of time for being outside or on the bridge sitting in the raised visitors chair watching seabirds and the great muscular-looking movement of jade coloured ocean swells. As a keen bird watcher, I took part in a Birds Tasmanian project identifying and counting the seabirds I saw. Volunteers were asked to take part on every voyage. Identifying albatross species was relatively easy, while identifying the many species of petrels, prions and shearwaters was far more challenging, especially the smaller prions as they look so similar and zip over the waves like inverted 'W' shaped arrow heads.

The Southern Ocean, which encircles Antarctica covers 32 million square kilometres, three quarters of which freezes during the colder months. That still leaves plenty of open ocean to cross and with little land to hinder the wind, seas are often whipped into dark angry foam-streaked maelstroms.

During the day, in mountainous following seas with the waves moving in the same direction as the ship, I would head to the trawl deck which is dominated by 2-metre-high drums of coiled hawser together with hydraulic winches, the stern open to the ocean. Just above the trawl deck is a stair platform, perfect for observation without getting soaked. At the stern I was confronted by a roiling boiling turmoil of ocean, the ships propellers churning and labouring to keep up and the deep thrum and vibration of the engines. An 8-metre-high wall of green water reared up behind the vessel, towering above the trawl deck roof, blocking out much of the light. The wave caught up with the ship and invaded the trawl deck, white water, neck high, swirling around the cable drums and submerging the winches. The 95-metre, 6,500-tonne ship was thrust relentlessly forward like a giant cork, riding the wave, the momentum causing the sea inside the trawl deck to peak forwards before the angle reversed as the ship climbed the next colossal wave and the water sluiced back into the ocean. The receding water gushed in great green torrents over the stern. The sight and sounds of this event were spectacular to observe knowing that the Big Orange Ship was built for ocean going conditions as well as for ice, because at times like that I could not help but wonder if she could cope in such tumultuous seas.

Figure 4: The aurora australis. This image was taken at sub-Antarctic Macquarie Island. Credit: © Dr Aleks Terauds.

Out on the open-air flying bridge at the witching hour under clear skies, conducting another midnight weather observation, shimmering curtains of green, sometimes red gossamer danced across the moonless sky. These were the southern lights, or aurora australis, after which the ship was named. The coloured spectral lights appeared and disappeared, rippling, meandering sheets stretching across the celestial dome and then fading before being renewed. At times it started slowly and built to a crescendo, a symphony of light. On other occasions it was fleeting, appearing and disappearing in moments. It was a vision splendid, sufficient to make me breathless and mute. I stood on the rolling deck, eyes to the sky in wonder. I enjoyed as much of this spectacle as possible because with every passing degree of latitude southward, the hours of darkness decreased. Once we broke 60-degrees south, the southern lights would be so much harder to see, and eventually become invisible in twilit nights.

In heaving seas and howling winds, close to the Antarctic Convergence, great scimitar birds were on the wing. Several species of albatross: black-brows, greyheads, light-mantled sooties, wanderers and royals. Their flight was like poetry in motion, they rode the wind with graceful ease: they are born to it. Watching them was mesmeric, a meditation of sorts. Their flight is parabolic. On stiff wings they soar high into the air and then dip low over massive swells and flying spume, wing tips almost grazing the waves. There were a couple of dozen great birds interspersed with their much smaller, faster cousins the prions, petrels and shearwaters. It was an aerial dance as though carefully choreographed. Seabirds were everywhere: straight ahead, behind, and glimpsed on all sides in my peripheral vision. They gloried in winds gale force and above, and in such conditions, the albatrosses rarely flapped their wings. I spent hours observing them and could never get enough, reluctant to go inside, even for meals.

The Antarctic Convergence is an area where the cold Antarctic waters meet the relatively warmer sub-Antarctic seas, the resultant mixing and upwelling bringing nutrients towards the surface. The

Figure 5: A wandering albatross with a 3-metre wingspan glides effortlessly over the ocean. Credit: © By JJ Harrison (https://tiny.jjharrison.com.au/t/fCEqOJC1cJUcoIOa) - Own work, CC BY-SA 3.0, https://commons.wikimedia.org/w/index.php?curid=18290910.

32-48-kilometre-wide convergence encircles Antarctica between the 48th and 61st parallels and is rich in marine life due to enormous phytoplankton blooms that are food for Antarctic krill. Krill, shrimp-like crustaceans, proliferate here and are the preferred food of whales, seals, seabirds including penguins, squid and fish. Hence the area around the Antarctic Convergence is often busy with feeding seabirds and marine mammals.

One dark moonless night on the flying bridge, weather observation almost concluded, I looked to the stern and gasped. The ships wake glowed neon green, like an alien landing strip a kilometre long. Looking down over the side, 14-metres to the water, bioluminescence sparked fiery green with the ships passage. Under a star-spangled sky I stood alone on a moving deck a thousand miles from anywhere, spellbound, witness to a light show created by trillions of tiny sea creatures: zooplankton. In daytime, two days later, and in calm seas, the ship ploughed through what looked like millions of boringly coloured dildoes. These long white, tube-like creatures were salps, planktic tunicates, highly efficient filter feeders, gorging on the season's first phytoplankton blooms. There were so many that the ocean appeared to be more gelatine than sea water. The spectacle went on all day until dark and no doubt beyond. Next day the swarm of salps was gone.

Six days into the voyage at about 58-degrees south, the water temperature was minus 1.8 degrees Celsius. There was a gently rolling sinuous swell; the seawater had become thick and cloudy and was smoking eerily all around the ship. This was grease ice which has the appearance of cooking oil spilled in water creating a milky appearance. The 'smoke' is the result of the water being warmer than the air. There are many names for sea ice, especially as it develops: frazil, grease, nilas, pancake and sheet ice. Sea ice formation can be gradual or rapid depending on conditions: the colder the water and the cooler the air near the surface, the faster it forms. Patches of newly formed nilas bump up against one another to form pancakes. Once the plate or platter sized pancakes fuse together, sheet ice forms. This is called new ice. With age, new ice becomes first year ice and then second year as well as the much thicker multi-year ice. First year and older ice is known as pack ice. What we had all around us in that moment were the beginnings of the frozen ocean, a spectacle that I had waited a lifetime to see.

The Orange Roughy steamed onwards, the air temperature falling with each passing day. The wind picked up and the sky was obscured, snow began to fall, swept along on a stiff breeze. Minus 10-degrees, time to break out the freezer suit, the padded jacket and over-pants, balaclavas and mitts. The Australian Antarctic Division issued us with good gear, no expense spared. Low quality clothing can mean hypothermia, leading to poor decision making, confusion and perhaps even death: a false economy by anyone's measure. Suitably clothed I climbed to the flying bridge on lookout for the first iceberg. We were carving our way through pancake ice that had begun to fuse together, the ships wake like an eight-lane highway, a clear passage through the developing ice sheet. I could smell tonight's dinner through the massive kitchen vents: fish and chips, yum! But I wasn't ready to go below. On every voyage to Antarctica there is an iceberg lottery; whomever sees the first iceberg wins a pot of money that is donated to charity. But there was no luck today, though I was thrilled that we were getting closer to the frozen continent and to the ship breaking ice.

A few days earlier we had passed the latitude of Macquarie Island at 51 degrees 30-minutes south: it is a place I long to go. The thin sliver of land, only 34 kilometres long and five kilometres wide, is a sub-Antarctic jewel, 1,500 kilometres east-south-east of Hobart, Tasmania. In spring and summer, it burgeons with wildlife: around four million seabirds (mostly penguins) and tens of thousands of seals. Four species of albatross breed there too, including the mighty wanderer that has the world's greatest wingspan. Macquarie Island is the fourth station managed by the AAD although the island itself, claimed as part of Tasmania, is managed by the Tasmanian Parks and Wildlife Service.

Next day a shout went up, someone on the bridge had spotted the first iceberg and the ship's master announced it over the tannoy: 'iceberg ahoy off the port bow'. The usually almost empty flying bridge became crowded with sightseers. Cameras clicked and camcorders whirred, this season's first iceberg was instantly famous. The lottery winner was announced with A$1600 to go to a children's cancer charity. Excitement over, folk drifted off and went below, only a handful remained. But where there is one iceberg there are generally more. On the bridge, iceberg watch began in earnest. Amidst this vast icy ocean, the *Aurora Australis* was a tiny floating platform, and our only life support system. Two thirds of the way from Hobart to East Antarctica there were no other vessels within thousands of kilometres that could, should we founder, come to our rescue. With up to nine-tenths of an iceberg below the water line they were now our deadly enemies.

Figure 6: The first iceberg that we saw was not that noteworthy or photogenic. This one was much further south amongst the pack ice and was one of many that we encountered as we proceeded towards Antarctica.

Although ice strengthened, the ship can only travel safely through pack ice up to 1.23 metres thick. Icebergs are made of much sterner stuff than sea ice, coming as they do from the land and not formed at sea. The ice that comprises an iceberg begins life high on the Antarctic plateau: snow is compacted to form ice which then flows in vast ice sheets to the sea. Calving from the terminal faces of the world's largest glaciers the icebergs drift northwards, some the size of an office block, others as big as towns, even cities. The massive ones, those that are 100-kilometres long or more are given names or, to be more accurate letters and numbers. These behemoths are tracked by satellite, in part so that shipping can avoid them, but also so that glaciologists can track and study them. One summer such a berg prevented tourist ships reaching Sir Douglas Mawson's old hut at Cape Denison, that is sited within the 42-percent of Antarctica claimed by Australia, far to the west of Casey station.

The freshwater ice of icebergs is far harder than concrete. Running into one at speed saw the demise of the RMS Titanic and hundreds of passengers and crew. Underwater the ice can skin a ship, in this case like peeling an orange. Bergy bits, also known as growlers, are an even more insidious hazard. These large chunks of ice, often weighing several tonnes, float just below the surface and are almost invisible.

Huge, enclosed lifeboat pods on board the *Aurora Australis* can each seat 70, with supplies for six weeks or more. Designed for both ice and ocean, in rough seas they roll badly. With only a small windscreen for the pilot and a bucket with a curtain across for the toilet, life inside can get ugly. The other deadly enemy at sea is fire and is potentially worse than striking an iceberg. All rooms and spaces are heat and smoke alarmed because a major fire on board can be catastrophic, especially in the engine room. Fire can spread quickly to engulf the ship and even if it only destroys the engine room the ship is left with no power to navigate or to heat the living spaces. It really does not bear thinking about. Hence there were emergency drills every Saturday morning: dry suits and life jackets were mandatory for these drills and if it was the real thing, you better be sure to be adequately clothed.

The ship was now breaking ice, albeit only 30-centimetres thick. I was at the bows, hanging over, looking down. Snow was falling steadily from a leaden sky; ice crunched underfoot and lay on the decks and the air felt dry and brittle. Ahead it was impossible to tell sky from ice. We had been joined by two dozen snow petrels: incredibly white birds with black beaks and legs. These are true Antarctic natives, breeding amongst ice free rocks on the continent and feeding largely amongst the pack ice. It was so good to see them: our Antarctic welcoming party, and an indicator of the continent's proximity although it was still a long way away.

Figure 7: The ships wake stretches into the distance as she easily carves a way through new pack ice on a beautiful day.

The prow of the ship cleaved the snow-covered ice and cracks appeared then shot forward like lightning bolts, either straight ahead or to left or right. Sometimes the cracks opened for hundreds of metres ahead as though pointing the way south. Snow petrels dipped into the open water, snatching crustaceans from the surface, easy prey for them and the reason that they accompanied us. I was out there at the bows for hours, entranced by the scenes around me. It wasn't just the ice that held me there: as we forged through patches of open water, Adélie penguins rode the ship's bow wave. These were my first Antarctic penguins and the ones that I was heading south to help research. They twisted and turned, porpoising with astounding agility off the waves, their underwater wakes like torpedo trails. They are indeed organic torpedoes, born to their liquid element just as ocean going seabirds are born to the wind. Their penguin black and white tuxedo colours were clearly visible as several birds crowded the bow wave. It was so good to see them that I whooped with joy.

Open water is also home to the great whales. Minkes surfaced and blew near the ship, gentle giants feeding on phytoplankton. They occur singly or roam in small groups several strong, their breath expelled like steam blown backwards on the breeze. Being up to eight metres long they wowed us all, the deck and bows lined with eager faces. Whale sightings were telegraphed around the ship so that all who wished to could see them. One day I missed a humpback breaching within metres of the ship as I was rushing to my cabin for my camera. I had forgotten my golden rule: experience first, pictures second. We miss so many experiences by staring through view finders or now at screens. Yes, we get the photo or video, but the real experience is lost. With senses fully engaged and remembering to breathe, an experience like a breaching whale is somehow imprinted on one's soul, forever remembered. It can be triggered by any similar image, and someone nearby has a photo of it anyway.

Months later, on our return journey, with more open water and less ice, it would seem like whales were everywhere. Most were not such spectacular sightings as breaching humpbacks, but rather distant views of whales spouting, gleaming black backs and dorsal fins sluicing water. I love it when they sound: tails raised high into the air, sliding slowly and inexorably into the mysterious oceanic depths. We saw Minkes, humpbacks, southern right whales, fins, mighty seis and blue whales. What is it about whales? I have never met anyone who does not love these gentle giants. It feels like a benediction when they appear, nature's blessing, the closer they get the higher the levels of excitement and awe. I'm a wildlife nut: all things wild I adore, although some, like mosquitoes, midges, march flies and leeches, I could happily do without. But they all have their place and play important ecological roles. Perhaps it is the whale's intelligence and their curiosity of ships and humans. And of course, the fact that for over 150-years they were wantonly slaughtered and yet now that the carnage is long over, they still want to be near us.

As we proceeded south, more and more icebergs appeared. They came in so many shapes and sizes. Some were quite plain and tabular while others were spectacularly blue with tall towers and incredible crenelations, cliffs and ridges, peaks and troughs, ledges and pinnacles. Some even had their own ice caves and grottoes. Icebergs may be at sea for years, slowly decaying, frozen into the sea ice during winter and then released during summer to once again roam storm-lashed seas on ocean currents. Strangely, the on-board excitement over icebergs had all but ceased and there were no more photographic frenzies, yet there were always a few stalwarts like me that could never get enough of icebergs or this rare polar adventure. We were often outside at the bows, the stern or on the flying bridge. Kindred souls. Solitary experiences in the wild have their own buzz and energy but to share them magnifies that pleasure. Those of us on board who were regularly outside, gravitated towards one another and chatted animatedly about our shared experiences. Yet on many occasions I was out there alone, happy in my solitude.

Having gone to bed after the midnight weather observation I was dreaming of bells tolling amidst a violent thunderstorm. I woke suddenly to a deep clanging and booming and at first was confused as to its origin. Then I realised: we were breaking ice through the night. I quietly got dressed, grabbed my outdoor gear in case it was needed and headed up to the bridge. I hadn't been asleep long, an hour at the most. On entering the bridge from the neon lit corridor, I paused, blurry eyed to gain my night vision. The bridge was rigged for night running, no bright overhead lights, only a desk lamp lowered over the curtained off chart table and further forward the eerie green light from the radar screens. I greeted the second mate, alone on duty, who was perched on his raised captain's chair, surrounded by instruments. The controls of the ship are ridiculously small, basically a knob to turn her great rudder and another for forward and reverse. The visitor's seat is a replica of the captain's chair, high and with excellent forward and port side views.

Two massive external search lights, one mounted each side of the bridge, juddered and shook as the ship's bow impacted the ice. This was first year ice about one-metre thick. The beams of the searchlights illuminated the ice ahead in a cone 500-metres wide and extending outward for more than a kilometre. In inclement weather these distances were foreshortened. It was snowing heavily that night, reducing vision to a few hundred metres. Below the bridge are the forward holds and around them all sorts of heavy machinery and shipping containers were chained to the deck. Beyond all that lies the bows, so the ice being broken was not immediately below us. Out in front, the ship seemed to devour the ice, the pack disappearing below the bows at a rapid rate and yet we were travelling at only 2.5 knots. The sound was incredible, deep rumbles, booms and clangs, the violent clamour that had entered my dreams. The front of the ship curves upwards so that its forward momentum and weight break the ice, the massive chunks rolling along beneath the hull,

19

crashing against it, turning the ice breakers thick steel plates into a dull sounding bell.

Long experience of sea ice conditions is essential to the crew when so deep into the Southern Ocean. Were we to be in desperate need of rescue it would be at least a week or two in coming. Explaining why a multi-million-dollar ship sank to its owners would be tricky, not to mention the 120-souls on board depending on getting safely to their destinations. No pressure then for the ships master, or his officers. But in the chair that night the second mate knew that icebergs were rare amongst first year ice, they are more prevalent and more dangerous in open water. But taking sea ice and icebergs for granted can make a fool out of anyone and result in disaster.

We stared ahead, searching for icebergs, the juddering lights making one's already strained vision difficult to focus. Thick white flakes were pouring down, momentarily dancing erratically on the air currents before being swept away to settle on the pack ice, the snow deepening. It was blown on the wind from left to right in front of our eyes. Illuminated by the searchlights the snow blurred into thick silver cables that moved up and down before me. Encased in the other worldly neon green glow of the radar screens, both of us were silent. The second mate remained alert, he had to be, while I, hypnotised by the wind driven snow, had gone within myself. We could have been on the moon or in outer space. I no longer felt part of my body, those silver cables constantly moving up and down on the wind were hypnotic. I didn't know how the officers on watch could remain immune, perhaps at times they did not. The green glow, the booming, crashing ice, the strain and rumble of the ship's engines, juddering lights streaming through thick snow, the pack ice ahead as it disappeared rapidly beneath the ship: all of it combined was overwhelming: other worldly. And yet I was totally at peace, mind empty, devoid of thought, floating in space, energy raised to a sublime level: an experience never to be forgotten.

Somehow, I came round, a particularly large chunk of ice striking the hull: BOOM! I had no idea how long I'd been out: half an hour, an hour? I felt so dreamy, body movement slow and relaxed. I said goodnight to the second mate and, preparing myself, exited the green capsule into blinding white light. Adjusting to the corridor glare quickly, I was off down the bright white human conduit: destination the stern. I had to see the chunks of broken ice emerge from under the hull, as though minced through a giant machine.

The trawl deck was always floodlit at night, the ship's wake illuminated in case someone should fall overboard. To get there from the bridge was a significant distance and descent. You can do so inside the ship or outside. I kitted up and exiting a sea door on the port side of the bridge, I crunched through patches of drifted snow along the deck and down several metal stairways to the helideck near the stern. I had no choice then but to descend internal stairs, C-deck to E-deck, through the wet lab to the noisy trawl deck. The ships engines and propellor thrummed loudly, moving us ever forwards, ever southwards. Two huge hydraulically operated cable drums sit side by side: the steel cable is for deploying and hauling nets and deep-water sampling rigs. I had to be careful as there was no guard rail at the stern: not a great way to go, crushed between blocks of ice and frozen to death in polar seas. The sight back there was literally awesome: great chunks of ice as large as a Land Rover rolling from beneath the hull up onto the surface, constantly turning as they were flushed backwards by the boiling wake. Blue ice glinted in the artificial light, shades of white and blue, the churning ocean aqua green. As the massive fragments of ice were flushed backwards, they appeared to attempt reassembly, their nature to be part of an ice sheet, not tumbling alone in the sea.

My last port of call was the railing at the rear of the helideck. From up there the ship's wake stretched away into the night. A broad swathe full of rolling, tumbling ice junks, snow covered ice sheets stretching out either side: making our own frozen ocean superhighway

During the day, watching the chunks of ice surface and rotate, what had been the underside of the ice was often stained brown. This I discovered was algae that grows on the ice and is an important food source for krill until the pack-ice breaks up and algal blooms become water-born. It was a surprise to me; ice and algae did not seem to be a natural fit. I realised how important pack-ice is in the Antarctic ecosystem, and what might happen should there be less of it due to climate change.

Ten days into the long voyage and there was thick multi-year ice ahead. To go around the barrier, even were it possible, could take days. At 140-kilometres from Casey station, near Petersen Bank, helicopters could shuttle to and from the station. With the ship at a standstill and everyone appropriately dressed for the minus 15-degrees cold, the first chopper's main rotor blades were reattached while in the hangar and then rolled outside onto the flight deck while the second machine was similarly equipped inside the hangar. Final checks were carried out and the first chopper was good to go. The Bureau of Meteorology staff at Casey were providing weather updates every half-hour in fine weather; every few minutes if visibility deteriorated on station. In a whiteout, even with sophisticated machines like these, flying becomes dangerous.

I stood at the railing just above the flight deck with several others, our excitement palpable, this event was not to be missed! That morning after breakfast the voyage leader had briefed us; mainly instructions and information for those flying to Casey, but also rules and exclusions on the flight deck and, for those just observing: no loose items of clothing allowed. In later years, outside areas of the ship were closed during flying operations with only pilots, engineers and those expeditioners being transported allowed outside.

Each helicopter carried several summer personnel and were packed with either fresh fruit and vegetables or mail bags. We looked down, only metres from the big red and white machines as the huge rotors began turning and spun up to a roar. The weight came off the suspension and with a great rush of air it rose vertically, turned through 45-degrees and with nose-down rose smoothly to a few hundred metres above the ice to wait for the second chopper which soon joined it. Together they banked around the ship and turned southwards, disappearing shockingly rapidly into the nexus between ice and pale blue sky. This would be the first physical contact with the outside world for several months at Casey, as it would be for all three Antarctic stations. The anticipation on station for fresh fruit and mail from home would be intense.

Figure 8: Thick pack ice stretches to the horizon on every side as the ship breaks ice towards Casey station. We stopped soon after as the ice became too thick for the ship to proceed.

In a couple of months' time, once the sea ice broke out, Casey would be resupplied, the crew that had been there for 12-months would be retrieved and the new winter crew deployed.

After a couple of hours, the choppers returned, and the process reversed; the rotor blades were removed, and the machines wheeled back into the hangar and strapped down. It was a professional and slick operation and soon we were on our way again, breaking ice towards Davis.

Satellite imagery, and the knowledge of how to interpret the images is crucial for ship navigators when amongst the pack ice. The various shades of white, grey and black on the screen depict the age of the ice as well as areas of open water. In this way the ship's captain and his officers choose their path through the ice. Gaps in the ice known as leads, allow optimum travel; the ship makes good time and uses less fuel. If the leads were conveniently joined up in one 1,400-kilometre-long canal through the ice, life would be easy for the captain and crew. The reality was quite different: sometimes hundreds of kilometres of pack ice were followed by leads of varying sizes, then more pack ice, or perhaps a narrow lead. It took an experienced captain to thread the needle. Older multi-year ice could be up to eight metres thick and had to be avoided. Only the massive nuclear powered American and Russian ice breakers could cut through that.

Another feature of the pack ice is polynyas. These are semi-permanent areas of open water, much larger than leads, generally found closer to the Antarctic continent and caused by wind, ocean currents and perhaps patches of warmer surface water. Polynyas are also found amongst the pack ice but can be unpredictable and hence leads are followed more than polynyas. Wind and ocean currents are big factors in the distribution of the pack ice and can result in large areas of open water, which herein are called leads.

On this leg of the voyage, marine science was conducted. The work took different forms, some was carried out in open water and some on the ice. On a calm blue-sky day, the vessel stopped beside a floe of stable pack ice and a crane cradle transferred scientists from the

Figure 9: Scientists deployed by crane cradle onto a stable icefloe. From left to right is the seal team, a photographer, the ice-core team and the ice depth and water sampling team. The pack ice may look easy for a person to traverse but pressure ridges and other features make crossing it very challenging.

ship to the floe. Ice cores were taken as well as water samples from beneath the ice. In addition, once suitably accessible crabeater seals had been spotted on ice floes through binoculars, two vets and four seal biologists were deployed. Dressed in white paper suits (over full kit) for camouflage, when clustered together on the ice, the team's peaked white hoods made them look like polar pixies. An experienced dart gun operator crept towards slumbering seals and if downwind was generally successful in darting them. Anaesthetised adult crabeater seals had satellite tracking devices that incorporated time-depth recorders attached to their backs using thick grey quick-set glue, while the vets monitored their vitals. The data from these devices provided data on the time, location and depths of dives of these pack ice specialists and their likely prey at those depths.

Crabeater seals are the most numerous seal species on the planet and are mostly solitary. The species breeds on ice floes spread across seven million square kilometres of pack-ice. Krill comprises 98% of their diet and they have specially adapted multi-lobed teeth for catching and sieving the five-to-six-centimetre-long crustaceans.

Often, when you see footage of killer whales hunting seals amongst Antarctic pack ice, crabeater seals are their target. With a seal on a small ice floe the orcas use their bulk to wash the animal off its icy perch. If unable to out-manoeuvre the killer whale pack, the seal becomes lunch.

Figure 10: A female crabeater seal on an icefloe. She is about 2.3-metres long and gets around by humping her bulk over the ice. Note the long narrow face which is due to crabeater seals primarily eating krill.

No sooner had the vessel stopped to deploy scientists on the ice, than a number of the world's tallest penguin appeared as if by magic. Walking in a stately line, several regal emperors waddled as elegantly as penguins can towards the ship. Stopping and looking up, necks craning, eyes shining, they regarded the Big Orange Ship, and the happy faces staring down at them with some interest and quite a lot of puzzlement.

They may have never seen the like before. I felt so thrilled to see them, our first emperors! Who knows where they had come from and yet groups of penguins (both Adélies and emperors) found the stationary vessel every time she stopped in the pack ice. I have an enduring love of penguins, and this mighty bird breeds through the Antarctic winter in conditions that no person could survive even for ten minutes. They have my utter respect and admiration.

In open water areas a conductivity, temperature, depth rig or CTD was deployed via cable winch. This large circular steel frame or rosette, a metre and a half tall, contains conductivity, temperature and depth sensors as well as up to 24-sample bottles that are automatically opened and closed to collect sea water at specific depths. I was on the trawl deck to watch the operation. Great care and attention were taken, the rig treated like a new-born. Data gained from the apparatus about water at various depths includes salinity, temperature, pressure, turbidity, fluorescence (via tiny zooplankton) and dissolved gases. Depths of up to 4,000-metres can be sampled.

Measuring salinity at various depths is particularly important as trillions of tonnes of colder, highly saline water, leaks into the ocean from the pack ice and sinks to the bottom. This colder, heavier water in turn drives the great oceanic conveyor belts; the currents. As the earth's climate warms, and ice melt increases due to our actions, the fear is that with less pack ice, these currents might slow down and eventually even reverse. This would have catastrophic consequences for life on our planet.

It took three weeks for the ship to travel 1,400 kilometres through the pack ice, stopping to conduct marine science programs along the way. Hour after hour, day after day, week after week in the frozen polar seas, breaking ice day and night or steaming along open water leads. The weather was highly varied: sometimes blue skies and high cloud followed by spectacular sunsets, while on other days there appeared to be no separation between ice and sky, just a homogenous pearly miasma or leaden skies. It often snowed, day and night, although there was little darkness now, only a few hours of twilight. On other days there were full blown blizzards, with masses of snowflakes being hurled violently out of the gloom, the ship doing 2.5 knots moving ever westwards, the clang and boom of ice on the hull now so familiar.

I was out there in all of it. I knew the value of being in the moment, especially in a place that totally confounds experience, there being no reference point from one's everyday life. It was a deeply humbling experience and one I might never have again.

We were perched on a tiny bright orange floating platform thousands of kilometres from the nearest city, the ship churning its way through a frozen sea so vast that it boggled the mind. And always we were subject to unpredictable polar weather. To have a cosy cabin and a hot shower, three great meals a day, tea, coffee and cake on tap anytime you want it, the correct gear to be out in any weather, and company whenever you desired it, what's not to like! Often, I was out there alone for hours. The odd person might keep me company or be out there somewhere too, but the solitude was fantastic. I found that situation to be the best kind of solitude, company when I felt the need and solitariness when I did not: I know of few experiences or opportunities quite like it.

On blizzard days, using the ships rails for forward momentum, I'd climb to the highest point on the vessel. Minus 20-degrees centigrade, minus 30 with wind chill. There I would be in full muffled gear, two balaclavas plus fur lined hat with ear flaps and face guard, a pair of ski goggles too; hands in two pairs of wool mitts plus heavy sledging mitts over the top; unrecognisable to anyone else, gender indiscernible; as anonymous as one can be. I'd lean into the icy blast, battered and buffeted, caked in snow and ice, the howling blizzard all around me, visibility sometimes cut to zero. I felt so energised and alive, so thrilled just to be there, living in the moment in a place that is hostile to human life.

One fine day, (I had lost count of the number of days out of Hobart and quite frankly I no longer cared), the captain and the AAD voyage leader decided to give us all an unforgettable treat and a welcome break from the monotony of weeks in the ice. We pulled up next to a massive stable ice floe, the sea door was opened, and the short gangplank lowered onto the ice. Ice anchors were installed to moor the ship to the floe, and we were free to leave the ship and cavort on the ice. It was

Figure 11: The three amigos: emperor penguins arrive to scrutinise the Big Orange Ship and its strange giant penguin-like occupants.

like seeing prisoners released onto a tropical island. Folk went wild, spontaneous snowball fights broke out, a football match commenced, cricket gear appeared from nowhere. We weren't permitted to go far from the ship in case weather conditions deteriorated or the ice floe showed signs of instability. But as on every other occasion when the *Aurora* stopped in the ice, the wildlife came to us.

Small mobs of Adélie penguins were the first to appear. Then, as though the word was out, more and more arrived, a long line of them waddling over the ice. The emperors came next in all their majesty and suddenly there I was on my knees surrounded by penguins; it was a long-held dream come true. Joy surged through me. Penguins are so zany, so characterful, so endearing and so immediate. Fights broke out in their eagerness to get closer. The first in a line of emperors stopped suddenly before me, the ones behind bumping into one another in a domino effect.

There was a blur of flippers as they whacked one another in annoyance, one or two falling over in the melee. Flippers and beaks were used to right themselves, looking bashful and embarrassed. There were sideways looks at me as if to say: 'we don't normally behave in this way'

On our way again, the deep thrum of the engines, the boom of broken ice on the hull. The familiar sounds of the last weeks restored. Three days later, on a fine calm day, steaming up an extensive lead, water glassy and reflective around us. Suddenly directly ahead the glistening black scimitar fins of killer whales rose from the depths, one dagger-like fin two-metres high. I was perched at the bows and felt my heart lift in excitement. Whale exhalations were blown mist-like high into the air, the sound like disconnecting a hydraulic air pressure lead, times eleven in this case: a bull, eight cows and two well grown calves. The call went out from the bridge, and the bows and the flying bridge became crowded, cameras galore. By the time they got to their positions, the whales had travelled several hundred metres, great gleaming fins and backs rising and submerging, rising and submerging, over and over, breathing with an explosive hiss on each occasion. Their black and white raiment was so distinctive, forever recognisable, especially under such clear water.

Figure 12: A scene from iceberg alley near Davis. Note the Adélie penguins on the small icefloe in the foreground.

As we approached another barrier of pack-ice the killer whales sounded, water dripping from great shining black tails as they dived and slid slowly into the depths. Gone. As though they had never been. The ship steamed on, breaking through the ice beneath which the orcas had vanished.

As we neared continental Antarctica, heading for Davis station, the *Aurora Australis* entered Iceberg Alley. Here the ocean floor can rise very quickly, from over 1,000-metres to just over 100-200-metres depth. In this region, within tens of kilometres of Davis Station, the seas are relatively shallow. This creates the ideal circumstance for icebergs to become grounded. In addition, shallower water often equals strong currents and so the fast ice is less stable and breaks out earlier than in deeper water. Hence the reason why Davis can be accessed earlier in the season while Casey and Mawson are still locked in.

The ship was surrounded by hundreds of shining, glinting towers of ice, many with spires and turrets, ice caves and overhangs, blue ice and green as well as opaque crystalline ice sculptures. There were one or two spectacular jade bergs, partly comprised of frozen sea water. Some icebergs showed the signs of having flipped over. This is a regular occurrence due to ice melt, the berg becomes unstable, one side heavier than the other and almost in slow motion, thousands of tonnes of ice, tips end over end. The resultant tidal wave of water can be enough to destabilise a ship as big as the *Aurora Australis*.

The scene in Iceberg Alley felt surreal, the Big Orange Ship, having broken ice to get there, gliding almost silently and ghost-like through calm glassy water that reflected puffy white clouds, the bergs all around, many towering high above the vessel. Snow petrels filled the air around us, eager for any crustaceans flushed to the surface by our passage. Ahead of us, Adélie penguins porpoised through the shimmering water, themselves coated in a shining aquatic film. It was at such times that I had to almost pinch myself to ensure it wasn't a dream, that I was really there.

The icebergs had most likely calved from the world's largest glacier, the Lambert Glacier, forty to eighty kilometres wide and four hundred kilometres long. It flows from the continent to terminate in 200-metre-high ice cliffs in Prydz Bay, to the west of Davis. The Station is 20-kilometres from the beginning of the icecap, across open rocky hills: the Vestfold Hills. This rocky, mostly ice-free region is bisected by fjords. Ice on the fjords provides excellent haul-out sites for Weddell seals to pup making it the perfect study site. There is one field hut on the plateau while six or seven others are located amongst the Vestfold Hills. One fjord, Deep Lake is so saline that the surface does not freeze during winter, even when temperatures are as low as minus 30-degrees.

In summer, with little ice and snow around the station it looks rather like a vast work camp. Davis is by far the busiest station for scientific work and with support staff and tradespeople it can house up to 120 people. It is the only station where helicopters, and or twin engine, ski equipped, Twin Otter aircraft are deployed for the summer, allowing flights to distant field camps or even between Davis and Mawson.

All too soon we had cruised through Iceberg Alley and were approaching Davis station through clear water containing brash ice - floating ice fragments up to two-metres in diameter. There was roughly one kilometre of fast ice (ice attached to the land) between the ship and shore and the captain expertly sidled the ship up to the edge of it. Contact with the station leader had been made well ahead of our arrival, especially as this was the station's annual resupply. The choppers were wheeled out once again and the rotor blades re-attached. As with Casey, the first helicopter flights carried fresh fruit and mail to the station. The ship's sea doors were opened, and the fast ice tested for safety and found to be at least 1.3 metres thick. Once it was declared safe for vehicles, ice anchors were laid to secure the ship and resupply operations began. With a short distance from ship to shore, the action was frenetic and unforgettable. The helicopters plied back and forth with netted loads slung beneath them while the ship's cranes loaded up trailers that were pulled by heavy vehicles across the ice back to station. Around four thousand tonnes of food, dry goods and other consumables were transferred to shore either by chopper or tractor. Loads of 200-litre drums of aviation fuel and petrol for quad bikes and generators were also flown ashore.

On the ship and onshore everyone pitched in to help. With fickle Antarctic weather, especially this early in the season, any window of opportunity had to be capitalised on. I got the chance to watch the action between periods of helping, and it really was a sight to behold. Only in the military can one witness an operation such as that. The big red and white twin-engine choppers came and went, massive down draughts of rotor beaten air rocking the spectators as they landed: the wocka-wocka thump of the main rotors adding to the drama. From my vantage point I was able to look into the eyes of the pilots as they brought the terrifyingly exciting machines into a hover right before me, ready to pick up another netted load. One chopper left while the next was soon in its place, hovering with another mighty rush of air. The noise was incredible. I should have been wearing earmuffs, but I was willing to take the risk, the full soundscape being far more thrilling.

Figure 13: A Sikorsky S76 helicopter returning to the ship for another load. This was taken during the Casey fly-off, but my enjoyment was the same as they came and went during the Davis resupply.

Meanwhile the vessel's big orange cranes swung back and forth, lifting metal cage pallets packed with goods and loaded shipping containers from deep in the ship's holds and lowering them onto the trailers, a few tonnes at a time. One tractor and trailer left as another arrived. This went on all day until 10 o' clock twilight, only pausing for helicopter refuelling and for lunch and dinner. Next day the diesel engineers were at work, an experienced team having been brought from Hobart for this specialist job. About 750,000 litres of special Antarctic blend diesel had to be pumped ashore: enough fuel for another year and a buffer amount in case extensive sea ice prevented ship access for longer next year. The fuel pipes, a kilometre or more long, were laid over the ice. Every joint was tested and retested, as in this pristine environment not a drop must be spilled.

Pumping of the fuel took 24-hours, the entire resupply operation taking about three days. All non-burnable rubbish was returned to Tasmania in cage pallets either for landfill or for recycling, and older vehicles that had been replaced with new ones were craned on board and lowered into the deep holds. The final act was for last winter's personnel to be flown to the ship and their luggage stowed. It was none too soon as a blizzard was forecast, and temperatures were falling. The holds were closed, and the cranes secured in their cradles. The choppers were once again mothballed in the hangar and the ice anchors retrieved. The ship's engines, silent for days except for power generators, roared into life. The captain used the bow thruster with the stern as a fulcrum against the ice, then put her into slow ahead, and we cleared the edge of the fast ice, now scored by a thousand vehicle tracks between the ship and station. He turned the Orange Roughy through 45-degrees and with several mighty blasts on the ships horn we were off, back out through Iceberg Alley, enroute to Mawson.

The primary colours of the big sheds of Davis station quickly faded to dots behind us and the first snow fell as the wind-speed increased.

Within an hour we were in white-out, howling winds and wreathed in falling snow. Perfect timing, as the ship was now clear of the hazard of Iceberg Alley. Soon we were once again breaking ice, the familiar rumble of the ship's engines reinstated in our psyches, the boom and bang of chunks of ice contacting the hull. I was alone at the bows again, everyone gone below to keep warm. Dinner would be in an hour, enough time for me to fully immerse myself in the soul searing Antarctic weather.

It was now 637 kilometres to Mawson, although it was unlikely that we would get closer than 100 kilometres due to predicted heavy pack-ice. I had to admit that even I would be glad to get there. Being confined to the ship for five weeks with only one brief release onto the ice had become a little wearing. However, with more time on ice floes, and a welcome change of environment, I would have been happy for the journey to continue indefinitely.

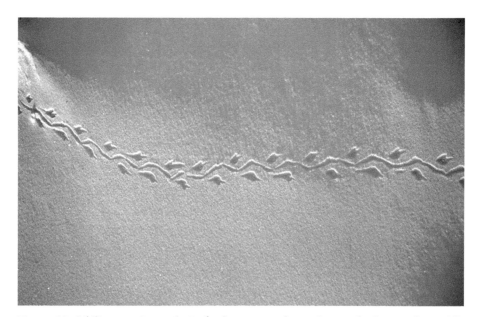

Figure 14: Adélie penguin tracks in fresh snow on the pack-ice. The line in the middle is made by the bird's long brush-like tail. I took the photograph by hanging out over the ships bows. I found the tracks so endearing and beautiful.

We made good time at first, finding some decent leads. I was looking down from the bows when several emperor penguins appeared, riding the ships bow wave, porpoising off the wave or zipping forward underwater with long tube-like wakes, so fast that it was almost impossible to follow them by eye. They hung around for a while, playing on the bow wave, and then were gone, off on another adventure. They seemed to take the sudden appearance of this large orange ship in their stride, even, though they may never have seen a ship before.

I was back to my old routine, out on the bows or up on the flying bridge. You may be thinking that I was a glutton for punishment, out in sub-zero conditions, but with warm gear to wear and a cosy cabin or ship's lounge below decks, there wasn't any real hardship. And because I spent so much time outside, senses open, years later as I write this, I am there again, so much so that I can almost taste it. You don't retain memories like that by staying inside and watching such wonders go by through the bridge windows.

Two hundred kilometres later the ice had grown thicker. We were breaking ice at the ship's limit when there was a deeper boom than usual, and the vessel began to turn to port and then slowed to a stop. We backed up, moved forward, backed up and moved forward again. This went on for an hour and then the ship finally stopped in the open water it had created. Rumours started to fly almost immediately just as in any small village. The captain and voyage leader called an emergency meeting in the mess. Apparently, a big lump of ice, known as a growler, had somehow impacted the rudder which was usually protected from such events. The rudder shaft was bent, and the ship could no longer sail straight. The vessel's owners and the Australian Antarctic Division had been informed and contingency plans were being discussed. There was talk that we might not get to Mawson, which was still 400-kilometres away, but may instead have to be towed all the way back to Australia. Those of us bound for Mawson felt distraught. We were so close and yet so far away. It was now a waiting game.

After the briefing there were still two hours until dinner and so I consoled myself regarding our situation by going on deck. As it had been for four weeks now, there was ice as far as I could see in every direction. Snow petrels flirted with the ship, looking for an easy meal, no doubt puzzled by the stationary vessel. It was always lovely to be in their company. The air was so dry that ice crystals fell from the sky like fairy dust, sparkling like billions of tiny diamonds in the muted sunlight. Half an hour before dinner I descended from the flying bridge to the bows. When I looked down there were two Weddell seals cavorting in the pool amongst the ice created by the ship. They whirled around and over one another, playfully nipping each other's tail flukes. It looked like sheer joy and a bond that went deep. There was nobody out there but me, and somehow, through the seal's playful presence I knew that all would be well and that we would get to Mawson. Watching seals play, especially such large, mottled beauties as these, was a magnificent gift and I stayed until the last moment, ten minutes before the dinner period ended.

The rumour mill went crazy: we were heading to Fremantle, no to Sydney, next the ship would be towed to dry docks in Southeast Asia. Round and round and up and down the rumours flowed. Eventually we got the news that the powers that be had decided on a long chopper flight to Mawson. Four hundred kilometres is close to the chopper's limit carrying full loads, and there would be a decision made at the halfway mark, the point of no return, as to whether to proceed or turn back. The aircraft could refuel at Mawson, so the success of the flight was wholly weather dependent. The Bureau of Meteorology in Hobart and the staff at Mawson coordinated to provide a forecast: it looked good next day. We packed our things that night so as to be ready at a moment's notice next morning after breakfast.

Next day, excitement levels were at fever pitch as the pilots finally got the green light. The choppers had been out of the hangar and ready for an hour and were now warming up. We all had to wear dry suits in case we crashed into the sea, with lots of dry clothes underneath, should we make an emergency landing on the pack ice or fast ice. The safety briefing seemed to last forever. After lots of waiting we were now being rushed, so we said quick goodbyes to shipboard friends and climbed aboard the helicopter. I couldn't quite believe that this was happening and that in a few hours we would be at Mawson, right on the edge of the Antarctic icecap. It was the end of one adventure and the beginning of another.

The aircraft doors were closed and locked, seat belts checked, and headsets put on. The rotors spun up and the cabin vibrated, the noise of the engines still very evident even with headphones on. We could see folk watching from the viewing platform as the weight came off the suspension and the chopper began to rise.

CHAPTER 2:

CHOPPER

O ur chopper rose vertically, hovered, then turned through 45-degrees before peeling away from the *RSV Aurora Australis* to await the second aircraft. Both of the two big red and white Sikorsky S76 helicopters were fully loaded with people, fresh fruit and vegetables, and the mail for Mawson.

Figure 15: The author about to climb aboard a helicopter on the ship's flight deck that is destined for Mawson. The big smile says it all!

I had mixed feelings about our departure: for the most part enormous excitement at the next leg of my adventure but also a pang of sorrow for leaving what had been my home for the last six weeks. The Big Orange Ship had brought me from Hobart, Tasmania across the wild Southern Ocean and into the frozen sea, breaking ice for weeks. We had travelled to within 140-kilometres of Casey station, broken ice to Davis and made it part way to Mawson. With a disabled rudder she would limp back to Australia. It was a sad end to a magnificent voyage.

We were fortunate to be flying to Mawson, our base for the Austral summer, as the decision to fly such a long distance may have gone the other way and we could have ended up returning to Davis instead. Our destination, Mawson station, is situated on the edge of Holme Bay on the Mawson Coast of Mac. Robertson Land, part of the 42% of Antarctica claimed by Australia.

The weather was fine: high cloud, low wind and no snow, perfect for flying. The pilot flew around the ship, waiting for the second chopper to join us. In Antarctica aircraft always fly in pairs for safety reasons, the region being so vast that a single downed chopper with a damaged emergency beacon might never be found. In addition, should one aircraft go down or make an emergency landing, those on board must be rescued immediately in case the weather deteriorates. Antarctica and its surrounding sea and fast ice are hostile environments for humans, and in blizzard conditions, with no shelter, survival may be measured in minutes.

We looked down on a vessel that had felt huge whilst on board, but now with elevation and a 360-degree view of her surroundings she looked tiny. It was a totally new perspective from the air and a humbling moment that brought gravity to the ship's predicament in having an unserviceable rudder. There was no end to the pack ice that stretched in every direction, a great white desert that encircles the continent. The situation reminded me of the early explorers in their fragile wooden ships and the incredible bravery of every one of them in the face of the unknown.

With the second chopper now in the air, the two aircraft made a final circuit of the ship, folk on board waving up at us madly, and then we turned south. I craned my neck and watched the *Aurora Australis* become an orange blob, then a speck before dissolving into the great white plain. What lay ahead of us was a mystery. Looking at photos, even video clips of Antarctica does not prepare you for the reality. Looking down on endless kilometres of frozen ocean, an iceberg here and there, it is a white wilderness like no other.

Figure 16: Looking back at the Big Orange Ship that is already beginning to look rather small amidst the vast icy wilderness. Credit: Wendy Pyper @AusAntarctic#AusAntarctic.

Flying at around 200-kilometres per hour it took only two hours to cross the vast icy wasteland to Mawson. Meanwhile, below us lay new and old pack-ice, fissures and pressure ridges, the odd slice of open water, and icebergs of various shapes and sizes.

At the end of the first hour there was rapid communication between the pilots and the Bureau of Meteorology weather observers at Mawson. The talk sounded like code, but the upshot was that the weather at Mawson was fine, and we could proceed with confidence to our destination. We had passed the point of no return.

Half an hour into our flight the sky had cleared to blue but after an hour an enormous cloud bank stretched across the horizon. At least that was my conclusion. I asked the pilot about the cloud, and he informed me with a grin in his voice that what we were looking at was the Antarctic ice cap. In that moment, the reality of the Antarctic continent struck home: its enormity truly magnificent but also rather daunting.

I can't comprehend a land area of 14.2 million square kilometres: my mind boggles. I have travelled around Australia, but Antarctica is almost twice its size, and during winter and early spring it is fringed by 20 million square kilometres of sea ice. It is not, as I once thought, a massive dome of ice with the pole on top. It is far more complex. Looking down from space directly above the geographic South Pole, one can see that the continent is unevenly distributed around the pole: the eastern half is much bigger covering roughly two thirds. In addition, the world's fourth longest mountain range, the Transantarctic mountains, divide it into two ice sheets: east and west, the East Antarctic ice sheet being the planet's largest. Even this is not a single dome of ice but a series of domes, ridges, plateaus, basins and valleys. Radar and satellite technology recently revealed that these features reflect the continent that lies beneath up to 2.5 kilometres of ice. Mountain ranges and peaks poke up through the ice sheets while others, some as extensive as the European alps, are buried beneath them.

Mawson station, in East Antarctica, is almost as far from the pole as one can get: 2,500 kilometres. A plateau rises to roughly 800 metres behind Mawson. Four ranges of mountains and a separate massif that comprise the Framne Mountains emerge from the ice. The ranges, which we could now just see from the helicopter, are oriented roughly north south and are between 10 and 20 kilometres apart. To the southeast of Mawson, 440-kilometres inland are the Prince Charles Mountains but beyond them there is nothing but ice.

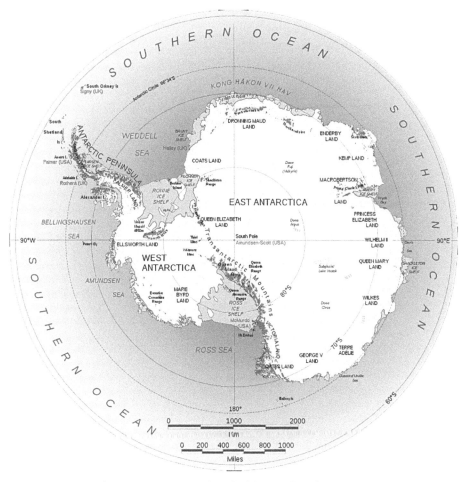

Figure 17: East and West Antarctica are largely delineated by the Transantarctic Mountains. The Antarctic Peninsula is prominent at top left and is the closest point to any other major land mass: South America. Only UK and USA stations are shown on this map. Mawson is on the coast of MacRobertson Land at top right, just below the words for 'Kemp Land'. Credit: Landsat Image Mosaic of Antarctica Team on Wikimedia Commons.

About 70 kilometres from Mawson, we crossed a stretch of open water, the delineation between pack ice and fast ice. There can be confusion about these types of ice because after all it is all frozen sea water and therefore sea ice. But while the pack ice drifts and moves around the continent with the prevailing currents and can be blown around by the wind, fast ice remains fixed in place (until it breaks up in the summer) and can be used for vehicular travel. Apart from the narrow stretch of sapphire blue water all we could see was ice, there was no sign of ice-free rock ahead and I wondered where the station could be located, hidden within this vast, icy world.

Closer to Mawson there were fields of scattered ice bergs that from 1200 metres up looked small, but from the level of the fast ice could

Figure 18: View from the helicopter on our approach to Mawson with the Antarctic plateau and the David Range of the Framne Mountains emerging from the icesheet. Mawson station is just visible at centre of image on the rocky promontory immediately below the plateau (look for the red and green shapes). The other rocky masses are some of the Holme Bay islands surrounded by fast ice. The West Bay ice cliffs and some crevasse fields can be seen to the right of the station.

be as big as half a dozen city blocks. These bergs were grounded on shoals (areas of elevated sea floor) and frozen into the ice in relatively shallow areas 100-200 metres in depth. That may seem deep, but icebergs extend downwards below the sea surface an exceptionally long way.

Around 30-kilometres from Mawson the pilot took us down to 500-metres elevation. Ahead and below us lay Holme Bay with a plethora of ice-free islands, nut brown against the white ice, the first dark colour we had seen in almost two hours. Beyond we could just make out the coloured specks that as we flew closer resolved into the big sheds of Mawson station, perched on what looked like a tiny area of ice-free rock. The polar icecap rose steeply behind the station to the Framne Mountains while sheer glacial ice cliffs marked the bays either side of Mawson.

My boss nudged me and pointed out two orange dots on one of the larger islands that were the living pods at Béchervaise Island field camp. That would be our home for the next few months.

Ahead lay Horseshoe Harbour, held as though in an embrace by two curving arms of rock, the western arm long and thin, the eastern one wider and slightly shorter. The harbour was, like the entire coastal zone: locked in ice. The station grew rapidly to dominate the forward view from the chopper, the name "MAWSON" spelled out on the row of massive black fuel tanks near to the shore.

Approaching the landing pad, the pilot said with some glee, in his thick Aussie accented voice, 'This lot haven't seen anyone new for months. Don't be surprised if they're like stunned mullets.' There was a slight pause and then he said, 'Welcome to Mawson!'. With great flair he brought the aircraft to a hover, right over the big letter H, and descending slowly we touched down without the slightest bump. We had arrived at Mawson. I was in Antarctica!

Figure 19: Mawson station from West Arm with the flat fast ice of Horseshoe Harbour in the midground and the icecap in the background. The black fuel tanks with the name 'Mawson' spelled out is just visible to the far left, almost hidden by a snow drift.

CHAPTER 3:

MAWSON

The welcoming party was buffeted by rotor wash as the chopper touched down. They looked like so many life-sized gnomes with long bushy beards: black, red or brown. Once the blades had ceased turning, we disembarked, so glad to have arrived. There were greetings all around before the crowd of winterers descended on the second chopper; the one carrying the fresh fruit.

Figure 20: Arrival! Both helicopters on the ground at Mawson. Hump Island is to the left and the ice cliffs of East Bay lie beyond. The cliffs are the terminal faces of the icesheet as it meets the coast having travelled thousands of kilometres from the interior.

It felt marvellous to be there and to be part of a great tradition: the Australian National Antarctic Research Expeditions, that was established in 1954. Over thirty years later my stay as a volunteer biologist was enabled and supported by the Australian Antarctic Division.

A four-wheel drive utility with a trailer arrived, and we bundled our luggage onto the back, followed by the mail sacks. Following the loaded vehicle, we walked as a group towards the large two storey red accommodation building known as the red shed.

Modern Australian Antarctic stations are a far cry from the early days. Mawson was Australia's first Antarctic station and indeed the first permanent base built on the continent. Constructed in 1954, the station was named after renowned Australian explorer Sir Douglas Mawson who was also the first to spot the ice-free granite-rock site from an aircraft in 1930. It must have been strange, arriving here on the ship and then having to build the kitchen and mess and what would become the accommodation building, whilst living in two oddly shaped insulated containers. Ten men and 27 huskies had arrived on the *Kista Dan*, a Danish polar charter ship, to raise the Australian flag. The ship brought all the building materials, some sections pre-made, two Auster aircraft for geographical survey and reconnaissance, and tracked snow vehicles called weasels from Hobart, together with a two-year supply of food.

Some of the original huts are still there. One of these, Biscoe hut, is the only wood framed and clad building ever built on an Australian Antarctic station. Mawson is a village compared to the town of Davis, yet it still covers several hectares and is comprised of about 60 buildings and converted shipping containers that are scattered across the site.

Figure 21: The massive red shed is in the centre of the image with the engine shed and new workshop (also red) to the right. The old workshop, known as the 'Rosella building' is left foreground near the shore of horseshoe bay. For a sense of scale, the yellow digger near shore is a 20-tonne excavator.

The new buildings, of which there are eight main ones, are huge, constructed of large modular externally insulated panels with colour bonded steel. Although the surrounding granite-like substrate is brown and there are many shades of blue and white, colour deprivation is an issue in Antarctica. Thus, newer building cladding tends to have strong primary colouring: post box red, forest green, canary yellow and royal blue. The red shed is enormous; around 12-metres high, 20-metres wide and 80-metres long. If you plonked the Big Orange Ship by its side, the vessel would only exceed it in size by a few metres.

All of the more recent station buildings are oriented in the direction of the prevailing east-south-easterly wind so that snow does not build up along their sides but instead is blown away. This also means that the access doors are on the exposed longer sides. Snow can still build up at either end of the buildings, in what is known as blizzard or 'blizz tails' especially at the northern end, but this is regularly removed by large front-end loaders.

We entered the red shed through a thick freezer door, removed several layers of outer clothing and then passed through another inner door to the interior. In doing so we had transitioned from minus 20 degrees to plus 25 degrees Centigrade, a 45-degree differential. Inside, expeditioners were walking around in shorts and tee shirts. It seemed so incongruous to arrive on the frozen continent only to see people wandering around indoors dressed for a tropical beach.

The fifteen men and one woman at the station had all over-wintered there and we were the first new faces for seven months. Despite this, although they were welcoming, we were not their primary concern.

Figure 22: The spacious bar and lounge area, upstairs in the red shed. Credit: Graham Cook.

Instead, their immediate interest was in the newly arrived fresh fruit as well as the parcels from home that included letters, gifts and audio tapes from wives, girlfriends, family and friends.

We were shown to our rooms and allowed some time for unpacking before the station leader gave us a tour of the red shed. Accommodation and ablutions are situated over both floors in the southern half of the building with laundry facilities at the far (southern) end. There is also a fully equipped surgery and operating suite on the ground floor. At the northern end, downstairs, is the mess and kitchen while directly above them upstairs is a bar, lounge, library and a movie theatre. Other facilities include a spa and sauna and a fully equipped dark room, both of which are downstairs.

As on the ship, life at Mawson revolved around mealtimes. There is chef-cooked food three times a day, the quality dependent on the ability of the cook but it is typically good. So long as Aussies got plenty of meat, especially steak accompanied by three veg they were happy and fortunately there seemed to be endless quantities. If you missed a mealtime there would always be leftovers in the fridge or you could cook your own meal, provided that you cleaned up afterwards.

There was internet access in most bedrooms as well as in the lounge and library. From the mid-to-late 1980s satellite communications revolutionised contact between expeditioners and their loved ones in Antarctica with a digital data service introduced in 1992. Communication in the 1950s and 1960s had been mainly by morse code with an allowance of forty words per month. If partners or family had lived near an Australian Broadcasting Corporation centre in one of the big cities, then a short radio conversation was sometimes possible. Now, with satellite communications, emails had become almost instantaneous, although letters and audio tapes from home were still highly valued. Other than computer games etc, indoor entertainment revolved around the bar with its dartboard and pool table, or the movie theatre stocked with hundreds of video tapes and DVD's.

The red shed has many windows. Each bedroom has one, but the much taller windows in the upstairs lounge area provide exceptional views: northwards over ice locked Horseshoe Harbour and beyond to the islands. Eastwards the view is of grounded icebergs and the shimmering blue ice cliffs that form the terminal face of the plateau ice sheet. Another window looks west over rock-strewn ground to the even higher ice cliffs of West Bay with the Casey Range rising from the icecap in the distance.

Unlike Casey and Davis, that are predominantly built on flat ground, Mawson sits on hilly ground interspersed with flatter areas. From a high point at the tank house and water supply building, one wanders downhill to the main flattish area where the red shed, main store, operations and communications building together with the geodesic satellite communications dome and the Meteorological sheds are located. A further descent takes you to the power houses, engineering workshops and vehicle storage sheds. Within a few metres of the shores of Horseshoe Harbour lies the fuel farm: two rows of huge black fuel tankers, each row comprised of eight tanks containing special Antarctic blend diesel. The fuel contains additives that allow usage in temperatures down to -50 degrees Centigrade.

Mawson's power supply for lights and heating is generated by three 125 kW diesel generators, the number of units used dependent on demand. There is a main powerhouse and one that is equipped with two generators that serves as a back-up in case of fire which otherwise could have catastrophic consequences for the expeditioners. The waste heat from the generators is captured to heat water which is then reticulated around the station buildings for central heating. Fresh water for drinking, cooking and ablutions is generated via a heat bell that is sunk into an ice cavern, situated in plateau ice just behind the station. Hot water is pumped through the bell to melt the glacial ice and it is then pumped into holding tanks in the tank house which in turn is fed to the station buildings.

Keeping the station running and fully serviced requires a team of electricians, plumbers, carpenters and diesel mechanics as well as communications engineers. During winter scientific staff include Bureau of Meteorology and upper air physics personnel, and on occasion penguin researchers. The station leader oversees and manages the personnel and makes any critical decisions often in conjunction with AAD managers in Hobart.

You can step back in time at Mawson just by opening the door to Biscoe hut, built in 1954. In there I imagined the men (because up until the 1980s all winterers were men) sitting around the mess table, post dinner, the hum of various conversations and laughter, the air thick with pipe and cigarette smoke. They wore woollen jumpers or tweed jackets and were comfortable without the 45-degree temperature differential to the outside world that was now the norm. I envied them that simplicity although I was soon to have a broadly similar lifestyle at our field camp on Béchervaise Island, bar the smoking of course.

From Biscoe hut one can call in at Australia's first modular insulated buildings with names like

Figure 23: Old and new huts (or sheds) at Mawson. Left foreground is the yellow electrical workshop leading to the green-roofed Biscoe hut. The aluminium clad hut in the centre is one of the first modular huts to be built at Mawson.

Wilkins, Shackleton, Ross and Dovers (all named for explorers or early expeditioners). Clad in shiny aluminium these were a mix of accommodation and store sheds as well as the electrical workshop. Even these buildings, also built in the mid-1950s, have less soul than the timber built and clad Biscoe hut. Other huts from that era have been removed: Law, Balleny and Fort Knox to name but a few.

For those like me who have an interest in aircraft, on the far shore of East Bay is a large hangar that once housed De Havilland Beavers and Austers. Built in 1956 the hangar was abandoned in 1963 following several crashed aircraft (fortunately with no loss of life) and one that had been destroyed in a blizzard. The fly boys mapped huge areas of East Antarctica that were until then unknown, virtually photographing them into existence. It must have been great fun in times long before occupational health and safety, flying by the seat of your pants over places never before seen by human eyes. The hangar, now empty of aircraft, echoed to my footsteps, and gave me the shivers, but I could imagine men busy with engine maintenance or opening the great doors onto the ice, hauling the ski equipped aircraft outside and the sound of their voices as they shouted instructions and shared lively banter between them.

Two of my favourite heritage buildings were Weddell hut, a carpenter's workshop (still in use) and the dog workshop that once housed the huskies' food, collars, harnesses and sled traces. Sadly, due to an environmental protocol, the huskies left Mawson in 1993 to be re-homed in Australia and Minnesota. But the smell of leather and linseed oil remain as well as the friendly odour of dog. The dogs' name plates are still there with names like Ursa, Morrie, Bonza, Elwood and Welf. One of the current winterers, who had been there back then, went on multi-week sled journeys over the fast ice and I was enraptured listening to his stories. The idea of riding a loaded sledge over the fast ice, hauled by eight or ten yapping, yelping huskies, all well known to the handler, yelling commands to keep them on track, and reaching faraway destinations, intrigued me enormously and I wished that the dogs were still there.

Finally, there was Weddell hut, known as 'chippie's chapel'. The entire pitched timber ceiling had been plastered with 1970s and 1980s Penthouse centrefolds. I believe that political correctness led to their removal in the early 2000s. After half an hour of gazing upwards, a crick in my neck, I exited the building, closing the door quietly in reverence.

On arrival at Mawson, all expeditioners must be 'field trained' by a qualified field training officer (who had arrived with us) prior to being allowed to travel beyond the station area limits which cover a 65-hectare area. Training takes three days and is conducted on the plateau. Fortunately, station limits include all of the ice-free rock, including the long rocky arms that designate Horseshoe Harbour leaving plenty of scope for exploration. Once field trained, my boss and I would be permitted to head out to our field camp.

While we waited to be field trained, we were schooled in the riding of quad motorbikes on ice. Four of us plus our teacher, the senior diesel mechanic (or dieso because everything gets shortened in Australia), black crash helmets on, UV visors down, rolled out onto Horseshoe Harbour. The harbour is roughly 90-metres deep, but a layer of ice between 1.5 and 2-metres thick makes it safe for vehicular travel, including for the much heavier all-terrain Hägglunds. The weather was calm and sunny, the temperature minus 20 degrees. I thought the training would be quite strict: I was wrong! In no time we were spinning donuts then gunning the machines and executing long sideways skids. We did get instruction to look out for snow drifts because hitting one in a sideways skid could result in a tip over and injury. Our teacher explained the hazard of tide cracks especially later in the season when the melt began, and they could be more than a metre wide. But mostly we just had incredibly mad, crazy fun, and once the session concluded we were deemed ready for unsupervised quad bike travel.

Saturday nights are made special on ANARE stations: a restaurant atmosphere is created, most folk dress in their finest attire, and the wine flows generously, the red glowing like rubies in the candlelight. With sumptuous food, pre-dinner drinks as well as the wine, conversation flowed more freely. Our arrival at Mawson coincided with a weekend and so on Saturday night we had the opportunity to get to know each other better, our individual roles and what life was like in our little polar village.

The trades people work Monday to Friday, while Saturday morning is set aside for station duties in which everyone plays a part. Inside the red shed and other buildings, corridors and common areas are vacuumed, swept or swabbed down depending on floor surface.

Figure 24: The welcome to Mawson sign near the end of West Arm at the entrance to Horseshoe Harbour, showing the stations map coordinates at 67 degrees, 36 minutes south and 62 degrees, 53 minutes east. The tip of Mount Henderson is just visible on the horizon.

Outside weekly tasks are conducted: burnable rubbish is incinerated, recyclables are sorted, and vehicles cleaned. If a blizzard has occurred blizz tails are removed from the northern end of the red shed and other buildings by front end loader. There is a weekly roster for kitchen helper, known as a 'slushy', assisting the chef in food preparation as well as washing pots and pans and manning the dishwasher. Another seven-day roster, named 'day-care', involves cleaning and tidying the bar and lounge areas. Each person does their own laundry using industrial washing machines and dryers. If you need soap powder, shampoo or toothbrushes and paste, or any personal items it's all available at the store shed appropriately named Wooley's. There is no need for money on station and indeed on returning to Hobart expeditioners often get called back by shopkeepers and restaurant owners for forgetting to pay.

It sounds like a cushy life but most folk work hard every day and it's the isolation from home that can be debilitating, especially during winter when the station is cut off from the world, ships and or aircraft being unable to access the station. In the 1950s and 1960s with only morse code messages the men knew that they were on their own for the duration, which somehow made their lives easier. Now with the internet and email, information that might once have taken weeks or months to get through is there in an instant. It can make for tough times should a relationship break-up or illness and bereavement occur back home.

In earlier days, the huge aircraft hangar was the venue for ball games but since the station re-building program of the mid 1980s and 1990s the massive green store shed was used for weekly badminton and volleyball games. There were also gym facilities in one of the old accommodation huts known as dongas. Otherwise, indoor recreation took place in the red shed.

During my six-month stay at Mawson, I was usually only on station for between one and three nights, when we came in from our field camp on Bech. The longest periods I spent there were on our arrival (prior to field training) and before I departed, during resupply. Other than the heating, which was set too high for me but was ideal for Aussies, it was an extremely comfortable environment. Having a drink at the bar, a game of pool or watching a movie were all a great treat. Internet and phone access meant I could keep in touch with my friends and family. The dark room would also prove invaluable and hot showers were like manna from heaven after a week or two of washing in a basin of water on Bech.

But my place was most definitely outside. I could only take the cloying heat of the red shed for so long. Inside I felt divorced from Antarctica, and other than having the views from the windows, especially those upstairs, I might have been anywhere. Awaiting field training, every day, all rugged up, I walked within station limits, revelling in just being there, walking on the ice of Horseshoe Harbour and out to the big sign near the end of West Arm that says: "It's Home, It's Mawson" with the latitude and longitude recorded beneath "67°36'S 62°52'E". From there I could see the summit of Mount Henderson, the closest mountain to Mawson, 20-kilometres away yet tantalisingly close. I was ready and eager for field training and the freedom that it would bring.

CHAPTER 4:

ANTARCTIC PLATEAU FIELD TRAINING

The Hägglunds' big diesel engine roared into life, the field training officer in the driver seat with three passengers, one up front and two behind. The bright yellow box-shaped rubber-tracked all-terrain vehicle, manufactured in Sweden, had a similarly boxy articulated trailer that contained tents and equipment for our three-day-two-night adventure. There were two other expeditioners riding quad bikes in convoy with us, making up a party of six.

Figure 25: The traverse-train trailer storage area at GWAMM. Kitchen, communications and accommodation units together with fuel drum sleds. The trailers are tilted due to ice movement and summer melt. Mount Henderson can be seen on the skyline between the first two trailers.

We were headed to the plateau about 500-700 metres above station and inland for around 25 kilometres. Mawson lies 150 kilometres within the Antarctic circle and its location on the continent means that it is almost as far from the pole as one can get. Any journey on foot, sledge or ski to the South Pole, old or new, generally begins (or began, in what is known as the heroic age) thousands of kilometres away from Mawson on one of two ice shelves: the Ross Ice Shelf close to the dividing line between East and West Antarctica or the Ronne-Filchner Ice Shelf in West Antarctica, both of which are bigger in area than the British Isles. From those two starting points the geographic south pole is roughly 1,300 kilometres away, 1,200 kilometres closer than if one started at Mawson.

The first part of our trip to the plateau was steeply uphill over a well-worn track of snow-covered ice, the all-terrain vehicle making easy work of it. Outside it was minus 22 degrees, calm and sunny, with the azure blue sky in sharp contrast to the blinding white snow. It felt great to be heading to the plateau and to be free of station limits.

After only two or three kilometres and at 150 metres elevation we came to a place known as GWAMM. I knew the name to be an acronym but for what, nobody seemed to know. Contact with the AAD revealed that the site was once used as an ice runway by the Royal Australian Airforce and the ground crew had named it using the first letter of each of their wives or girlfriends' Christian names. The catch was that nobody knew what the names were, so in idle moments I used my imagination, coming up with a wide variety of results.

GWAMM is the storage area for the inland traverse vehicles; fully insulated cabins mounted on trailers with skids that provide accommodation as well as kitchen and mess facilities to those travelling inland. There were also large skid-equipped fuel trailers designed to carry 200-litre drums of special Antarctic blend diesel. Huge D9 bulldozers were used to haul the trailer-train and I imagined them heading off on a traverse into the great white yonder, trundling along at about 10 kilometres per hour, deep into the interior, every day further from station. Travelling far beyond the coastal mountains was almost beyond imagining, there is nothing out there but a vast plain of ice in shades of blue and white. The strong primary colour of the trailers helps to reduce colour deprivation for the traverse teams and also to aid in locating them from the air should rescue be required.

We had a brief stop at GWAMM, to appreciate the views that were already exceptional: out over the islands and the flat expanse of fast ice of Holme Bay and beyond to the horizon, icebergs dotted here and there. The station was just visible far below us; its diminutive size an indicator of how rapidly we had ascended. Inland Mount Henderson (or Hendo in local parlance) rose majestically, its northern ridge seeming to be only a few kilometres away. Hendo is part of the Framne Mountains, yet it does not qualify as a range and instead is called a massif - a principal mountain mass.

Our training had already begun, the field training officer (driver, teacher and guide all wrapped into one) explaining to us that while we had a beautifully calm, clear day on which to travel, conditions could rapidly change. He explained that although sophisticated weather satellites and forecasting models meant that field parties could generally avoid being in the field during extended blizzards, the Antarctic weather can surprise even the most experienced expeditioner. Therefore, vehicles travelling on the plateau must follow marked routes, called drum or cane lines, in order to get from station to each one of the three plateau field huts at Hendo, Rumdoodle and Fang Peak without getting lost. Markers on these routes are comprised of rock-filled 200-litre fuel drums (the empty fuel drums providing a renewable resource for this purpose) with a four-metre-long bamboo cane through the middle and lodged in the blue ice underneath. The Hägglund's radar picks up each marker, set about 500 metres apart, that are also way-marked on the vehicle's GPS unit. This system makes travel by Hägglunds, even in a blizzard, safe, and with practice straight forward.

At GWAMM the cane lines diverge, both still heading upwards but with one route leading south-east to Hendo and the other southwards out over the ice to the North Masson Range and beyond. After quickly exploring the traverse vans, we climbed back aboard the Hägg and headed off uphill again. Our ascent to the plateau was not like climbing a topographically uniform hill; we would climb for a while and then the terrain would level out and then another hill or ridge of ice would take us higher to yet another relatively level area. We crested the plateau at around the 380-metre mark, and it was then that the sheer scale of our surroundings became evident. My mind struggled to comprehend it and failed, as what had seemed quite close in the crisp, clear air was in fact much farther away. To our left we could see the Mount Henderson massif, the furthest east of the mountain formations. The closest part of the Hendo massif is about 10 kilometres from the station, and it extends southwards for another seven kilometres to Fischer Nunatak (a nunatak is an isolated peak surrounded by ice).

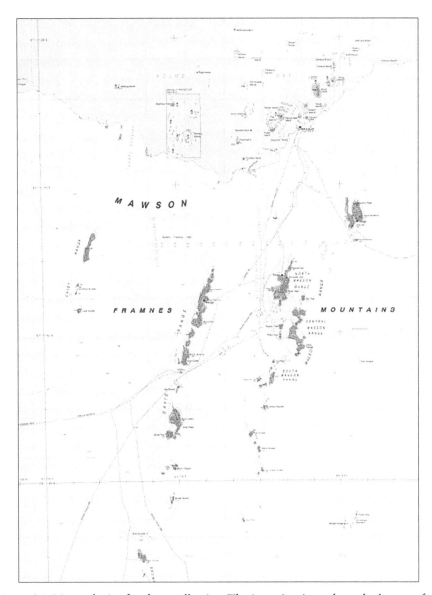

Figure 26: My apologies for the small print. The intention is to show the layout of the Framne Mountains. The ranges are, from left to right: Casey, David, Masson (north, central and south) and top right the Mount Henderson massif. Furthest south, in a line with the David Range is part of the fourth range, the Brown Range. The dotted lines are the cane line routes that all begin on the coast at Mawson. The map shows the distribution of the Holme Bay islands and their proximity to the station. Credit: Australian Antarctic Division on Wikimedia Commons.

Looking westwards (to our right), the distance from the Hendo massif to the northern end of the Masson Range is about 10 kilometres. From there it is a further 8-10 kilometres across the ice westwards to the David Range which is the longest of the four ranges. Following the line of the David Range southwards (inland) one comes to the Brown Range, about 60 kilometres from where we currently were. The Brown Range is separated from the southern end of the David Range by 20 kilometres. The Casey Range is located furthest to the west, about 20 kilometres beyond the David Range and 50 kilometres in total from Hendo. Like Hendo, the Casey Range is closer to the coast than the other ranges at around 10 kilometres (please see the map of the Framne Mountains on a previous page).

Figure 27: The kind of view that we experienced when on the Antarctic plateau: mountains and nunataks emerging through the 400-700-metre-thick icesheet. The highest peak, Mount Hordern is on the horizon at centre left.

The principal mountain heights are in the 900 to 1,400 metre range above sea level but only the top 400-500 metres poke through the ice which is between 400 metres and 800 metres thick depending on how far inland one goes (for example the ice is roughly 400-metres thick at Hendo hut, 500-metres at Rumdoodle and 700-metres at Fang). Moving inland, over a distance of about 1,200-kilometres the icesheet continues to rise in stages to a long ridge at about 3.5-kilometres elevation. It is along this roughly 3,500-kilometre ridge that East Antarctica's four major ice domes lie, the highest, Dome A being 4-kilometres high. By comparison the geographic South Pole is at 2.8-kilometres elevation.

Most of East Antarctica, including the Framne Mountains, lie beneath ice that is over 500,000 years old. It is notable that if all of the many trillions of tonnes of ice that comprise the East Antarctic icesheet was suddenly removed, the land below it would slowly rebound, rising upwards by hundreds of metres. This is known as isostatic rebound.

Between and all around the mountain ranges and nunataks that emerge from the ice are vast rolling plains of blue glacial ice and blinding white snow slopes and drifts. There were a few puffy white clouds in the sky and their shadows seemed to play on the ice.

I found that for me the best way of understanding the Framne mountains was to envisage mountain ranges without snow or ice: in other words, a relatively normal landscape that for me would be the Scottish Cairngorms or the Lake District mountains. Then I imagined it snowing continuously for a thousand years until the valleys and even the lower hills had disappeared and only the top third of the mountains remained visible. Then only the spines of the highest peaks would be showing, making the ranges look fragmented. The outlying peaks would become nunataks and therefore one would have a landscape similar to the Framne Mountains.

I asked our driver if we could stop and get out to have a proper look at our surroundings and he gladly agreed. The inside of a Hägglunds is comfortable enough but the design is mainly functional. With all of our bulky clothing on it felt rather claustrophobic. The thrum of the engine and the rumble of the heavy-duty rubber tracks over dimpled blue ice made conversation difficult. The windscreen and side windows are adequate, but it was nothing like being outside in the open air.

We all climbed out and the training officer turned off the engine. Silence seemed to flood in all around us. For a moment everyone was speechless, stunned by our surroundings that were like nothing we had ever experienced. The human brain naturally seeks to compare a new experience to others they have had, but in this case, there was nothing to compare it with. We were on the edge of a vast plain of glacial ice that was contoured into rolling hills and wide valleys with lines of jagged mountains on either side. Inland of our position the increase in elevation southwards appeared less pronounced than our climb to the plateau but I knew from the experiences of others at Mawson (and Antarctic literature on the subject) that when on the icecap one's eyes can be easily deceived.

The wind-scoured ice beneath our feet was not smooth, instead it was sculpted by the wind into dimples or wave like structures similar to a sandy beach that has been contoured by the tide. It was very slippery and in order to remain upright and maintain traction we had chains attached to our boots.

The plateau icesheet appeared white or a very pale blue depending on the light. I could generally distinguish wind-scoured ice from patches of blinding white snow that mainly occurred on or close to the mountains, often in huge drifts or snow-covered ice slopes that climbed the brown rock almost to the summit.

Polarised wrap-around sunglasses or goggles are essential in Antarctica, especially when the sun is at or near its zenith. Take them off at that time and you physically flinch away from the searing light. It quite literally hurts because 90% of the sunlight that is directed at snow or white ice is reflected. How those early explorers coped with their rudimentary home-made snow goggles I don't know. I have never experienced snow blindness, but I have suffered from a welding 'flash'; a momentary lapse while arc welding leading to seeing the intense light given off by the welding. It was not until evening that my eyes felt as though they were full of hot gravel, and I believe that time spent staring at a snow-or ice-covered landscape with the naked eye has a similar effect.

Having had a good look around we climbed back aboard our vehicles and engines started roared off over the ice plain towards the North Masson's.

About 20 minutes later we reached the partially crushed and twisted wreckage of an old Russian plane. We all piled out to have a look.

Figure 28: The belly-up wreckage of the Russian aircraft. The katabatic wind and blizzards have filled the fuselage with hard packed snow and also packed it in underneath. Credit: Craig Hayhow.

The Lisinov Li-2 (a Russian version of the DC3) crashed on take-off from the Rumdoodle ice runway in 1965 when a gust of wind lifted one wing causing it to crash into a crevasse. Nobody was hurt but the starboard wing and propeller were severely damaged. That same year a blizzard flipped it over and since then the ice has partially claimed it. The aircraft is still moving at about 30-metres per year towards the coast in flowing glacial blue ice. In around 70 years it should reach the coast, not far from the station.

The Rumdoodle ice runway, known as a ski-way, was utilised a great deal in the 1960s and 1970s, especially by the Russians (then known as Soviets). It is still used occasionally by ski-quipped Twin-Otter aircraft flying between Davis and Mawson. The ski-way is situated on the eastern side of the North Masson's near their northern end and planes took off towards the coast.

The Lisinov's tail fin towered above us, the fuselage part military green, part ice and wind ablated shiny alloy. The dashboard with broken dials stared back with empty black sockets and the fuselage, where men once sat, was full of hard packed snow. It was a reminder of times past and the friendship between nations in Antarctica, that in 1965 was missing in the industrial world. The International Geo-Physical Year, 1957-1958, was a huge scientific project involving 67 countries that saw great scientific cooperation between nations in Antarctica, including the superpowers that were embroiled in the cold war. It led to the Antarctic Treaty of 1959 which froze all territorial claims to the continent and called for the use of Antarctica for peaceful purposes and scientific research. The treaty remains a shining example of international cooperation and peace.

Having had many photo opportunities and a good look at the wreck we returned to the vehicle and the engine roared to life. For most vehicles the dimpled ice would prove difficult to traverse but the rubber tracks of the Hägglunds all-terrain vehicle provided us with a comfortable ride. The vehicle could negotiate just about anything including the fast ice, where if it were to break through it would float. At least that was the theory.

Figure 29: Part of the North Masson Range with the yellow Hägglunds at 200-metres distance already looking small. Two yellow-clad figures can be seen at right.

We soon reached the northern end of the North Masson's and following the cane line we travelled parallel to the nut-brown granite range. We stopped for another look around and I walked a couple of hundred metres away from the vehicle and was amazed by the impact of being such a small distance away. Two of them dressed in yellow looked like ants on the surface of the ice. I felt the lure of the mountains that lay beyond them, rising high into the crisp Antarctic air and framed by the most beautiful azure blue sky. What would it be like standing on the summit of one of those peaks and looking all around?

We continued on our way along the flank of the North Masson's, passing the turn-off for Rumdoodle hut and instead motoring towards

Figure 30: Polar pyramid tents set up on firm snow in the North Masson Range. Snow blocks weigh down the tent 'skirts' against strong wind.

the southern end of the range. The Masson's are divided up into north, central and south due to large areas of ice separating them. As I mentioned previously without 600 metres of ice, they would be one continuous mountain range.

We pulled up near the base of a 200-metre-long snow-covered ice tail tilted upwards at about a 30-degree angle and almost reaching the mountain's summit. Nearby, the slope levelled out and we chose the site for our camp. After hauling the gear out of the Hägglunds trailer we stood around dumfounded by our surroundings. The scale is epic, nearby mountains seeming to be only two or three kilometres away when in fact they are 10 kilometres away. But we could not stand around gawping, we had polar pyramid tents to erect, the same design as used by Scott in 1911. Unlike his tents, ours were brightly coloured post-box red and canary yellow. The colours on the plateau are dark chocolate granite (the rock is really charnockite gneiss, but it is granitic in structure), white snow, blue ice and bluer sky. To that we added the only primary colours on the plateau: the yellow Hägglunds and trailer, our brightly coloured tents and our red, yellow and green clothing.

Later when I walked a kilometre away from camp over the ice, I appreciated the colours even more. Without them it would have been difficult to find my way back even in such fine weather and excellent visibility.

Once the tents were up, we cut snow blocks using an ice saw and placed them on the tent's side skirts to weigh them down against strong wind. I felt quietly thrilled: this is what Scott, Amundsen and Shackleton did almost 100 years ago. I was on the Antarctic plateau and camping just as they did. Well, apart from the five-seasons sleeping bags, the high-tech clothing and high-pressure fuel stoves. But it was as close as I would ever get. With our sleeping gear laid out in the tents, we were shown basic climbing knots and how to rope up. With crampons attached to our boots and an ice axe each we headed half-way up the snow slope. The Field Training Officer demonstrated an ice axe arrest and gave us important pointers. Basically, once you begin to slide, turn on your front keeping your crampons away from the snow or ice and fall on your ice axe without impaling yourself. And don't let the pointy end of the handle catapult you into the air!

Figure 31: Cross-country skiing practice near our camp on the Antarctic plateau. There are no ski tracks because the wind sculpted snow is so firm.

Sounds easy, doesn't it? But after practicing the manoeuvre it got easier and then it became almost automatic. What it would be like with a real fall is anyone's guess. It could also be used to arrest one's descent into a crevasse, or that of a companion. It was great fun and where better to learn the technique than on the Antarctic plateau!

After some map navigation exercises, we did cross country skiing, mostly close to camp. My experience was limited, downhill skiing was more my bag, but at least I had done some cross country while two others had not. The training officer showed us the classic cross country skiing style over snow, skis shoulder width apart, pushing forward on each ski with assistance from the poles. The skating style is more difficult, pushing off on the ski poles and driving outwards on one's skis in a V-shape. The latter requires hard edges on blue ice in order to gain traction and was therefore more energy intensive. I would later need both styles for crossing the fast ice to Bech as some areas were eroded by the strong winds, leaving large patches of smooth blue ice.

We were shown, and then attempted, telemark turns on the snow slope, a difficult manoeuvre that I never quite mastered. I managed a 50-percent success rate which wasn't bad. Herringboning uphill came next and I did well at that, climbing high up the snow slope in a similar style to skating, only to realise that I then had to get down again. Skiing straight down would be dangerous with blue ice below, and therefore not an option. With a moderate strike rate at turning, most of my descent was done on my ass or sliding down on my side.

We cooked dinner, pleasantly tired from our day, and relived some of the whackier moments, the tumbles and falls and doing the splits on skis. We sat around enjoying our meal while the setting sun turned the three-billion-year-old granite mountains golden, and the blue ice seemed to glow from within.

Figure 32: Like a snap frozen wind-riffled lake surface, the wind scoured plateau ice requires crampons or boot chains for walking. We were joined by a quad biking companion too. Two nunataks are in the background.

As twilight approached, two of us decided to ski over the ice before bed, a good way to stay warm. The FTO gave us a handheld radio and instructions on what to do if any difficulty arose. Even going a short distance in Antarctica can be problematic should an injury occur, and therefore vehicles are used for travel over longer distances rather than walking or on skis: it can be a matter of survival.

The plateau ice looks like a snap frozen lake surface that had been choppy from the wind. Ripples, dimples and wavelets made skiing over the terrain hard work. We managed two kilometres, but after a day of exercise we were tired. We removed the skis and walked around to maintain warmth. From two kilometres away we could only just make out the colours of camp. In twilight the mountains were dark brown, the ice pale blue, stretching in rolling hills to infinity. The sky shaded from midnight blue to mauve and violet as the twilight deepened.

There was no sound. When I held my breath, I could hear the whoosh of arterial blood as my heart valves opened and closed. Absolute silence: not a breath of wind nor a bird call. Before humans came here the silence was total. Now, nearer station one could hear the thump of the big diesel generators that provide heat and light. It seemed ironic that some of that power was for freezers. But on the icecap, miles from anywhere, it was as it has been for hundreds of thousands of years, silent and immense, ice beneath our feet for as far as we could see, stretching inland to the pole. In Antarctica the silence enters one's soul, I had never experienced anything like it. In most places back home there is an aircraft flying overhead, the sound of a distant truck or motorbike, a barking dog, bird song or animal calls. Standing there on our skis in the twilight haze, the sheer enormity of the silence struck me as being other worldly, the kind of silence that most people would never know.

We were driven back to camp partly due to tiredness but mainly because a breeze had sprung up. I found it remarkable that at minus 20 degrees, even minus 25, in calm conditions I felt very comfortable in my high-tech polar clothing and yet as soon as a breeze began it felt as though a freezer fan had been turned on. In such conditions any unprotected skin began to freeze and removing gloves led to extremely cold fingers that required immediate warming. I learned that the super dry air of Antarctica and low temperatures by themselves were fine but add a breeze and it cut through you unless you added further face and hand protection.

Later, snuggled in my sleeping bag, wearing all my clothes, my ear pressed close to the ice, from far below came primeval music. Deep pings, booms and groans rang out as rivers of ice flowed downhill to the coast. The true nature of ice, its plasticity, hit home. It was not a solid immovable block but something almost alive. The icebergs I had seen hundreds of miles to the north came from a place like this, calving after a thousand years of travel to the sea. Standing on the ice I could not see the glacial flow lines, for that you need elevation. I knew that from the peak above me the flow of the ice was evident, billions of tonnes of ice constantly on the move. I tried to remain awake and to listen to the incredible sounds, as though mythical giants were battling each other far below, but being weary after a long day, sleep soon claimed me.

Leaving camp next morning we travelled by Hägglunds over to a small nunatak, about 130 metres high. Winds of up to 200-kilometres per hour scour out deep troughs in the ice around the southern end of any obstacle. Cliffs up to 70 metres high remain unseen until one is right above them. This was todays first lesson: beware of the southern end of mountains and nunataks, death lurks there over sudden drops.

The cliffs near our chosen nunatak were only 40-metres high, but even so, as someone who dislikes exposed vertical faces, I was hoping that we weren't going down there. Sadly, for me the plan was to abseil down and then climb back up using prusik loops and hand-held devices that grip the rope. Ice climbing would have been an easier option, but as novices we were not qualified and had no previous training in that technique.

The training officer demonstrated the installation of ice anchors and how to rope up using harnesses and carabiners. Three days of field training in the highlands of Tasmania prior to our departure had somewhat prepared us: we knew how to abseil safely and how to prusik using loops of chord as well as ascending devices.

As I shuffled back towards the edge of the abyss our guide said 'lean back, it will be easier' which was okay for him to say with his alpine and Himalayan experience and a cool head for heights. With trembling knees and gulping air close to panic I did as instructed and slowly passed over what to me was the lip of hell. Face to face with the blue ice cliff, crampons skittering over a surface that barely chipped under sharpened points, I remembered to breathe. Taking several deep breaths after my initial terror, I did what does not, nor ever has come naturally to me: to trust in the gear and the FTO's anchors. I had been told not to look down but that's impossible: I looked down. Aaaagh! It took a few moments to regain some kind of equilibrium albeit a terrified one. Slowly, kicking off the ice I lowered myself down, with great encouragement from those below. Done without fear and with confidence, a descent like that can be fast and fun. I tried my best to enjoy it, but I was as ever on any abseil relieved to be down, on solid ice rather than solid ground.

Once we were all down, we walked along the scour, imagining the incredible winds and the thousands of years that it took to create this deep bowl that from the ice cliff sloped back up to plateau level at the northern (seaward) end of the nunatak. We were tiny ant-like creatures next to the ice cliffs and the towering brown spire of rock. And there were many nunataks and ice cliffs that were larger than this one.

Ascending the 40 metres of ice cliff was exhausting. But once in a rhythm it went well: pull up the foot loops and step in, then push up the palm grips and repeat. On and on, up and up, face close to the ancient blue ice. Climbing up it was easier not to look down, but I still did so and felt my guts churn. I reminded myself that this was a one-off experience and tried to enjoy it, but my legs trembled, nonetheless. The air was so dry that breath did not condense instead turning immediately to ice on my short beard.

I felt so relieved to top-out, and that was followed by elation. I had done it; I'd conquered my fear and not disgraced myself. That old chestnut: male pride, the need to prove oneself and not back down can be deadly, yet I was glad that I had done it. What an adventure!

Figure 33: Wind scours like this one at the southern end of nunataks on the polar plateau are truly incredible and potentially very dangerous when nearing them from above. They provide great ice climbing for those that like that kind of thing!

Feeling the sweat on my back rapidly cooling I shrugged on a padded jacket having climbed only in my freezer suit. In sub-zero conditions, especially when there is wind, hypothermia is a killer. Decision making becomes confused leading to mistakes that cost lives, so we were constantly reminded to look out for the signs in our companions: the mumbles, fumbles, stumbles and grumbles. Frostbite is another hazard, and we were repeatedly drilled during field training that teamwork is essential with regular checks for white (frozen) skin patches especially on the cheeks and nose. Fingers could also be frost-nipped when gloves were taken off for even the shortest time.

After Packing up the climbing gear we piled into the Hägglunds and or mounted quad bikes and re-joined the cane-line route and motored across the ice to the David Range. To reach Fang Peak hut one enters an almost hidden valley in the northern end of the range between a large crag and Fang Peak itself. The bright red hut suddenly came into view on our right and we motored right up to the hut which sleeps four. We gathered together and the training officer took us through the procedure for arrival at a hut: turning on the gas and power, clearing any snow from the door as well as from the hut's air vents. He explained that the latter could save our lives because without snow-free vents carbon monoxide from the gas stove and heater could build up inside the hut and lead to the occupants getting headaches and feeling drowsy. That in turn led folk to lying down on their bunks perhaps never to wake up again. All of the huts are insulated pre-fabs with a freezer door and double-glazed windows, so ventilation is essential.

Figure 34: Arrival at Fang Peak hut and the chat from the training officer about air vents and hut safety. Note the view through the gap to the Central Masson's.

Soon the kettle was on, and chicken noodles and mugs of tea and coffee prepared. Food always tastes so great in the outdoors or when staying in a tent or a hut. There was relative silence as we all tucked in. While drinking a second hot drink our teacher explained hut etiquette: always leaving a hut spick and span ready for the next occupants and of course remembering to turn off the gas and power. Leaking gas is dangerous and the loss of precious gas due to leaks at field huts can mean having to resupply it so that the hut can continue to be used.

The view from Fang Peak hut's window is confined by the valley entrance but in the crystal-clear air we looked across the ice plain to the Central Masson Range. Sated with food and drink I lay back on a bunk for a few moments to 'rest my eyes'. I was jolted awake by the others moving, fifteen minutes had passed as I dozed. Collecting ropes and carabiners from the Hägg we headed for the nearby granite crag. On the mountain's craggy lower slopes, we practiced rock climbing: three points of contact our mantra. The granite is fissured and rough, providing great hand and foot holds. A single pitch, the rock laid back at a friendly angle, my love of scrambling came to the fore. There's quite a lot of yelling involved in climbing, the person above shouting out and then the climber below shouting 'ready' and then 'climbing!' We abseiled back down and then repeated the performance. After the sheer face of the ice cliff, I felt more secure on the rock although I used a lot of energy being tense rather than relaxed which the training officer regularly reminded me of.

Back at the hut, another cuppa in hand, our guide took us through blizzard survival skills. The golden rule is DON'T PANIC! Panic leads to poor decisions and possible disaster. Take some breaths, try to remain calm, and come up with a plan. In a group, designate a leader and follow them. Any plan must remain flexible.

Figure 35: A blizzard on station. The photo was taken in what passes for good visibility in a blizzard, total whiteout rapidly followed. The large grey golf-ball-like structure is the geodesic dome that protects the stations satellite communications dish.

On station there are rope lines between the red shed and the other buildings or places of work. The 'blizz' lines are held at waist height by metre long steel pitons secured in the rock. Blizzards result in periods of zero visibility and with wind chill the temperature may be as low as minus 40 degrees Celsius. Losing your way can mean death. With the help of blizz lines station personnel can travel to and from their workplaces safely. Even so, each person must carry a radio and call in before going out and on arrival.

If a blizzard hits while on the plateau, a party must seek shelter immediately. If in a Hägglunds vehicle, and as long as the engine keeps running, you are safe. Using the radar, the driver can navigate the drum line to a hut or back to station, preferably the latter as blizzards can last for days. If caught out on quad bikes, on foot or on skis, it can quickly become a matter of survival. Australian Antarctic Division policy states that nobody should be out in the field by themselves;

always travel in pairs. If you can't make it to a field hut or back to station you must find shelter, preferably by creating a snow cave. Hiding behind rocks or, if on the fast ice behind an iceberg is temporary, if hypothermia sets in your survival may hang by a thread.

We were drilled in how to navigate back to a hut or station on quad bikes in a blizzard and what to do if caught out whilst travelling shorter distances on foot or on skis. It all sounded rather dire with survival the aim and the continual mantra of 'don't panic!'

With the training officer's talk complete we piled into the Hägg and were off back to camp in the North Masson's: not for us the comfort of a hut! Our driver was chatty, the passengers silent, perhaps like me they were digesting the recent information. Listening to the training officer, this place became one big field of danger when in fact, provided one followed certain rules, it was reasonably safe.

Tired after a day of exercise, and having burned more than a little nervous energy, my thoughts tended towards dinner and bed. But as

Figure 36: In the Framne Mountains, on top of Antarctica, not far from camp. Utter quiet and endless space.

is often the case a good feed revived and reinvigorated me, and so I headed off alone, a little way up the hillside.

People are all different and thank goodness for that. Some would hate this place: the profound silence could literally drive those who need constant sound or chatter mad and the isolation from loved ones would be prohibitive. For many, the cold would be punishing and for others the lack of colour stimulation and the mind-bending vastness would be forbidding. For me, the reality of Antarctica was beyond my wildest dreams, and I could not get enough of it. The comforts of the red shed were marvellous, but it was not why I had come. I was there because the Antarctic wilderness is like no other place on earth, nothing even comes close. And I wanted to absorb it and to make it part of my being; my soul if you like.

After an active day in the company of others I needed stillness and solitude and this place provided the opportunity for both in great abundance. In deepening twilight, I sat high on the hillside looking out over the icecap and mountain ranges. My surroundings were beyond stunning, the enormity of the place blew me away. I had a feeling of expansion within me, and I hoped that it would always be there. The sky graded from dark blue to indigo and violet and the darkened granite stood out almost purple against the milky blue ice. An hour later I headed back to camp. Once again, I tried to stay awake to listen to the glacial machinations far below, but again I slid inexorably into sleep.

Next morning post breakfast, tents and gear packed away, we had a last ski. I practiced blue ice skating, the method that I would use on the eroded fast ice between base and Béchervaise Island. My boss had already said that she would walk, cross country skiing not being her thing. But for me it was the best form of travel and I looked forward to the challenge.

Ski practice over, we chugged back past the North Masson's, our eventual destination being the station. The training officer pulled up near the crashed Russian plane, which lies on the edge of an extensive crevasse field. We roped up to practice traversing crevasses as well as simulating crevasse rescue. Our teacher demonstrated screwing in ice anchors again; practice makes perfect! Properly secured we traversed the ice field and our guide pointed out what to look for: snow packed fissures and bridges that for the uninitiated look suitable to walk on. He bent down

Figure 37: A volunteer inside a small crevasse. Credit: Tsylos Michael F. Coyle (Blue Toque) on Wikimedia Commons.

near such a spot and using a long pole bashed at the snow which collapsed into a yawning chasm that appeared to have no bottom. He got the response that he was hoping for: a gasp of abject horror at yet another potentially terrifying demise in Antarctica. Strangely the chasm drew me in, the sheer scale of it excitingly tantalising and the colours: blues, indigoes and deep violets, so like last night's twilight sky.

I breathed a sigh of relief, though, when someone else volunteered to be the crevasse victim. The team used their ice axes and crampons to arrest the volunteers-controlled fall, in lieu of the real thing. Then the volunteer used prusik loops to climb back out. Seeing them in the crevasse I couldn't help imagining the demise of Douglas Mawson's travelling companion Belgrave Ninnis who in December 1912 disappeared into a massive crevasse with a fully loaded sledge and his dog team, never to be seen again. His friends mourned his loss as well as the food supplies for their journey that were on the lost sledge. As a result of great hardship, lack of food and because they were forced to eat dog livers, high in vitamin A, Xavier Mertz perished about three weeks later. Only Mawson survived and returned, half dead, to the coastal hut only to see the ship leaving, condemned to remain another winter at Cape Denison, deemed the windiest place on earth.

Our crevasse volunteer told us that it was a far different experience being in one than looking down into it from above, the sheer ice walls appearing to lean inwards as if they might close over his head. He also said that he never wanted to fall into one because from what he could see there was no bottom, just a black gaping hole. It was also another reminder of the constant movement of ice from the pole to the ocean. We were looking down on ice that formed on the high plateau perhaps a million years previously, an incredible thought.

Crevasse rescue complete, we reloaded the equipment in the Hägglunds and set off for station, crossing the ice plain towards Hendo. The last three days and two nights had opened my eyes to the mind-boggling scale and stunning beauty of Antarctica, but also about how hostile it can be to humans. I had learnt how wind can cut through blue ice to create scours up to 60 metres deep and discovered the devastating power of blizzards. I had gained so many insights into the nature of the polar icecap including the movement of the ice sheet and how its surface varied. I had learnt how important teamwork is as well as not panicking in adversity. I had also learnt that with sensible caution my time in Antarctica could be glorious.

CHAPTER 5:

BECH: ARRIVAL AND FIRST EGG

T wo days after our return from field training, we were driven in a Hägglunds four kilometres northwest to Béchervaise Island field camp, all our luggage and equipment in the trailer.

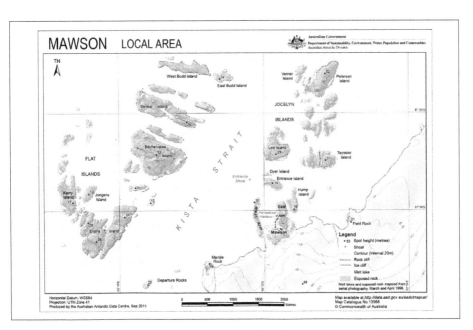

Figure 38: Béchervaise Island is the largest of the Flat Islands northwest of Mawson station across Kista Strait. A long narrow unnamed island lies between it and Stinear Island to its north. The shape of the harbour at Mawson, and the long thin promontory of West Arm is visible. Credit: Australian Antarctic Division.

The journey took us over Kista Strait, named after the vessel *Kista Dan* that had brought the first over-winter team to Mawson in 1954. Bech (pronounced Baysh), as the island is affectionately known and less of a mouthful, is shaped like a squat pear that is skewed to one side at its smaller (northern) end. It's about one kilometre long north to south and 700-metres at its widest, with a central ridge running from south-east to north-west and a summit at 47 metres which does not sound much, but in the Flat Islands of which Bech is the largest, any elevation counts. The field camp and the Adélie penguin rookery are situated at the flatter north-eastern end.

Three kilometres out from base our driver took us through the channel between Stinear Island and a long thin unnamed island that lay between us and Bech. He navigated past a smallish, block-of-flats-sized tabular iceberg lodged in the ice. Once clear of the channel, our approach to Bech was from the north, the all-terrain Hägg doing a big loop and then rolling up onto the island and straight into camp. The sun was low in the sky, casting long shadows, and making the Hägg, the rock and the living pods glow.

Bech field camp is a vision from an alien world. Two bright orange oval space-age looking pods, each eight metres in diameter, appear to

Figure 39: Arrival on Bech on a beautiful spring evening, temperature minus 20 degrees. Two large, grounded icebergs can be seen in the background.

have landed in ready-made steel cradles only a metre off the ground. The fibreglass-built pods or smarties (some call them googies, as in egg), were specifically designed for Antarctic conditions, their aerodynamic shape means that blizzards are unhindered, and snow cannot accumulate around them. Thick insulation makes them easy to heat, creating comfortable living quarters.

After turning the gas and power on, I climbed the metal stairs and unlatched the door that opens upwards, stepping inside my new home for the first time. Naturally, the space is very oval, the four windows too: it was like returning to the womb. The layout is excellent: a central round wooden table with tucked away chairs; at the northern end is the gas cooking stove with lots of space for pots, pans, crockery, cutlery, and the food items used most regularly, like cereal and condiments. There are also storage cupboards on either side of the cooking zone. The entire under-floor area is divided into four large storage bins accessed by hatches, and this is where our food supply and other consumables were stored. A gas heater is situated near floor level to the right of the cooker area; an ideal placement when one is seated at the table. Three bunks have storage areas both behind and underneath them. Above each bunk is a window. I could see that it would make a great home and that I would be far more in touch with the outdoor environment than on station.

As the season progressed, and the sun no longer set, we stuck thick black plastic sheets over the windows in order to help us sleep. In the land of the midnight sun, it was tempting to cut down on sleep in order to be outside, but over time this can lead to both mental and physical exhaustion.

The second pod is an office with plenty of room for equipment and a six-metre container is the equipment store shed. An apple hut provides excess storage space and there's a timber built dunny. All buildings are strapped down with substantial steel cables, anchored in the rock, to prevent their destruction by hurricane force winds. Being swept across the ice in an unsecured outhouse by 200-kilometre winds would not only be embarrassing and but also highly dangerous!

Power comes from storage batteries fed by solar panels and a wind generator, while the cooking and heating gas is from 95-kilogram bottles located outside. The field camp is resupplied every year by Hägg, using the fast ice as a highway, while larger items are brought in by helicopter during resupply. Ice from pressure ridges that are common around the islands, pushed up into hillocks by the tides, is melted on the stove and then stored in twenty litre plastic containers. Apart from plateau ice melted for drinking this was the purest water imaginable.

Figure 40: Proximity of the Adélie penguin rookery to the field camp at Bech's north-eastern end. Many islands and the odd distant iceberg can be seen amongst the fast ice in the background.

Every week or two we travelled over the ice to station to do laundry and have blissful hot showers as well as chef cooked food. We would stay one or two nights, then head back. The Adélie breeding schedule allowed us to have time away from Bech to go to other places such as the plateau field huts and Auster emperor penguin rookery 60-kilometres to the east. The fast ice does not last forever. It begins to melt in December, but the surface goes through many melt-refreeze cycles before finally being rotten enough to be swept out to sea, usually in late January. Then we used inflatable boats and the steel work boat, stored on station in a large boatshed, to access the island.

For most of our stay we were guaranteed sub-zero temperatures; in October often down to -20 degrees but by late December temperatures would be not far below zero. In these conditions everything not in a heated environment is frozen, including in the space under the living pod's floor. This has positive ramifications for human waste which must be carried to station for incineration. Being frozen solid there is no odour.

It was mid- October, and the first male Adélie penguins would soon be arriving. Every day my supervisor and I scanned the fast ice to the

Figure 41: The first male Adélie penguins arrive at Bech after having walked and tobogganed about 70 kilometres over the fast ice. They were literally running towards the island!

north, hoping to see some tiny black and white specks. A few days later I was exiting the dunny when I caught a movement from the corner of my eye. I ran and grabbed my binoculars. Far out on the white plain a small group of Adélies were literally running towards me, eager to reach the island and to claim a nest site. I did a little dance and shouted to my boss to come and see. We whooped and high fived, the male birds were coming!

Five 70-centimetre-high, black and white tuxedo clad penguins, the season's first birds, flippers outstretched waddled and tobogganed to the island, having crossed about 70-kilometres of fast ice, mostly non-stop. They paused near the shore and stretched their necks this way and that to check out the two intruders. We seemed to pass the test and they hopped and waddled on up to the rookery. The influx of Adélie penguins had begun!

Studying any animal species can be intrusive, often causing distress to individuals (and groups). The human's need to understand must be tempered by balanced judgement, the data often benefitting the species in the long-term. With an Antarctic krill fishery taking a hundred thousand tonnes of the shrimp like crustaceans that are also essential food for many marine birds (Adélie penguins included) and mammals, understanding how the fishery might impact them is crucial. Thus, the weight of known individual adult penguins returning to breed and then going back and forth to sea to feed their chicks is of great interest as it reveals their initial breeding weight and then how much food they return with each time throughout the breeding season. To gain this information manually would require a lot of handling of the birds, with high stress levels being inevitable.

An ingenious method was developed and introduced in 1990 to reduce invasive techniques and is used both on Bech and on Verner Island a few kilometres to the east (and now on many more islands by other nations). Birds have a rice-grain sized transponder, like those used for domestic cats, inserted under the skin on their back. An electronic weighbridge was installed on the main penguin access route, natural rock features and low fences being used to funnel the birds over it. On each side of the weighbridge are infrared sensors that read each penguin's tag, noting the direction the bird is travelling; either into the rookery or away from it. There is purposely only space for one bird at a time on the scales and so all birds are weighed (tagged or otherwise) every time they cross the weighbridge, throughout the breeding season. In this way, once the tag is inserted, there is no further need to handle the penguins, the data collated providing most of the information required including the length of foraging trips.

Figure 42: Adélie penguins crossing the weighbridge from the rookery on Bech. The rear penguin has just hopped onto the scales. The open rectangular metal structures at either side are the electronic tag readers.

The trickle of male Adéies arriving on the island became a flood, with long lines of birds stretched out over the ice. Within a few days the once silent empty rookery was inhabited by roughly 2,000 busy, noisy birds. The serious business of nest building was in full swing, the nest being made out of carefully selected stones from the size of an almond to a large walnut, although far more angular in nature (there is no vegetation for nest building in Antarctica). The most prized stones are around four-to-five-centimetres long and two-to-three-centimetres wide. Stones are important because they assist in nest drainage: snow melt following blizzards can chill eggs, killing the embryo within. The nests are therefore arranged in clusters or lines on sites with at least half-decent drainage, the stones often elevating the eggs above the melt water. Hence the more stones the better as far as Adélie penguins are concerned.

Figure 43: An adult Adélie penguin on its nest of stones. At least four other nests can be seen close-by. Note the powerful bill, the long brush-like tail and the white eye-ring that is used in intraspecific communication (towards each other).

The distribution of the nests creates colonies within the overall rookery or breeding site, Bech having 18 colonies. The best nest sites are within the colonies rather than on the edges. Internal nest sites are more secure from predator attack by south polar skuas (like a large brown gull in size and demeanour) and, generally inhabited by older, more experienced birds who are also more dominant. The older birds also arrive at the island earlier than younger ones to claim the best nest sites.

Adélie penguins, like many other penguin species, are social breeders, partly due to there being few suitable ice-free areas for nesting but mainly because of avian predators, there being safety in numbers. The nest site and a small area around it comprise the Adélie's territory which is vigorously defended against other Adélies or perceived threats from avian predators, mainly skuas.

Naturally, with so many nests in close proximity there are tensions and disagreements between neighbours. The Adélie penguin's weapons are its powerful beak and its bony flippers. "Flying" underwater at eight kilometres per hour makes for highly developed breast muscles and a whack from their flippers leaves one in no doubt about their intentions. The Adélie's beak can inflict serious wounds and is only used as a last resort. Adélies, like most social penguins, do not go straight on the attack but instead use their short crest and distinctive white eye patches in a series of gestures that are easily missed unless one knows what to look for. Beak pointing: the head with the crest raised is pointed directly at the threat. This is often followed by a side-stare or double side-stare. Beak gaping: opening the beak wide to show the pinkish-red interior of their mouth and throat that has comb like structures inside to aid in the capture of krill. This is used to intimidate others together with loud braying. These gestures can be delivered while the bird is lying down but if the threat does not abate, then the Adélie stands up and rushes at the intruder, breast thrust out, flippers and crest extended, and its head stretched high. They will take on anything or anybody to protect their nest and territory using their flippers and beak to great effect, sometimes drawing blood.

Stones for nest building are in short supply and they are worth fighting for. Stone stealing is rampant and sitting watching I wondered how specific birds would ever create a nest as every time their back was turned their neighbour stole their stones. But what goes around comes around: the thief was caught, given a good seeing to and then sent packing, still standing tall but with feathers sleeked and flippers held tight by his side, cowed and disgraced. At least until the next time. Some nests (usually those of younger birds) are rudimentary while experienced birds generally create substantial ones.

Figure 44: This male Adélie is performing the ecstatic display above the colony where all the females can see him.

Once the nest is built to the owner's satisfaction, he plants his large, webbed feet, opens his flippers wide, throws back his head, beak to the sky, and crows his ownership to the world, flippers flapping up and down in time to the vocals. This is known as the 'ecstatic display' and is a magnificent sight, with many other males across the rookery following suit: stating their claim and their readiness to mate.

The call is remarkable: it is a cross between a bray and a crow, hard edged and yet it is music to the ears of those who love them. If written the call would be: 'ka ka ka ka ka ka - ka ka ka ka ka ka!' Most penguin species (there are 18 species, all in the southern hemisphere) have a similar call including gentoos, macaronis, royals and rockhoppers. Only emperor and king penguins employ more complex trumpeting calls.

With most of the male Adélies present (there are always stragglers) and the nests built, the wait for the females commenced and the island seemed to hold its breath in anticipation.

My main job on Bech was assisting in the twice daily monitoring of 200 marked Adélie penguin nests, noting nest occupancy including whether both birds were present. While our focus was on the study nests, we also conducted rookery-wide observations which consisted of the total number of breeding pairs, the date that the first egg was laid and, once the egg laying period was concluded, the number of nests with eggs. Similarly, we recorded the date that the first chick hatched and later the number of nests with chicks as well as the total number of chicks present. The final count, conducted just before we left Bech in February, was the total number of chicks that were in crèches.

Male and female Adélie penguins are very similar in size and the only accurate way to determine their sex is by looking up their cloaca using a speculum and counting the number of polyp-like structures therein, a procedure that for some reason is not popular amongst penguins! Although technically it is possible to sex them based on beak size (the males having slightly more chunky beaks), this method is often unreliable. We knew that we could rely on the males arriving first and the females second, males mating with females were easily identifiable, and obviously only females lay eggs. Beyond that, with two birds at the nest who's-who can be a guessing game. However, with transponder tags specific to each bird, their age, sex and often parentage was known and the tag readers on the weighbridge removed any guesswork.

We scanned the northern horizon every day, waiting for the female Adélies to arrive. We couldn't predict with any accuracy when they would turn up, although data suggested that they would do so within a few days of the males' arrival. I could only imagine the expectancy of the males because every day that the females did not come, our own anticipation increased, and we talked of little else.

I was lucky to be out checking the horizon when the first females appeared far out on the ice, hurrying towards the island. I called to my boss, and we watched through binoculars as they approached just as the males had done, with great eagerness and urgency. When the sex hormones increase in spring, there is no denying the call to breed, and Adélies answer in their millions all around the icy continent (a total of approximately 3.8 million breeding pairs). For Adélie penguins, only ice-free rock will do, and they generally return to the island of their birth to breed – known as natal or nest site fidelity.

Just like their mates up in the rookery, the four-to-six-kilogram females arrived looking fat and healthy, their fronts gleaming in the sunlight, flippers outstretched, determination in their waddling stride, their longish tails brushing the ice at each step. Many folk think that penguins have short legs. Not so. Their skeletal remains bely the myth: their legs are in fact well-proportioned but because their life is at sea, only their ankles and feet emerge from their bodies, making them aerodynamically efficient under water. This confining 'skirt' is what makes them waddle. If they could lift their skirts, one would see legs not so dissimilar to ours: they would, if they could, run very like you and me.

The females stopped to check us out, giving us time to warmly greet them, and then hurried on up to the rookery, stopping to listen for the voice of their mate from last year, or for a new one. The boys had clocked the girls a kilometre away and were all displaying on or near their carefully prepared nest, the braying and crowing reaching fever pitch, their excitement at the arrival of the first females clear. 'Pick me, pick me' the strident voices seemed to cry.

The established penguin pairs had likely not seen each other in months but could distinguish one another's voice. First time breeders or those that had lost their previous mate were also there to meet their new beaus. The males puffed out their chests to accentuate their size and crowed loudly while displaying their wares: the nest of stones. Adélies are only partly monogamous, sticking with the same mate if they had successfully procreated in previous years. In the case of females, if their mate fails

Figure 45: An adult Adélie penguin. Note how little of the beak is free of feathers and the short crest at the back of its head that is used in intra-specific communication.

to arrive at the rookery, perhaps having been killed by predators or dying at sea, she will take a new mate. It has also been found that both eggs in a nest may not always be fertilised by their mate, perhaps for the females this is a way of hedging one's genetic bets.

Once they find their mate the females move swiftly, hopping over the rocky ground on both feet at once, heads held high and flippers by their sides in a submissive pose. Identity is quickly established and then comes the sweetest of ceremonies, known as the mutual display. Both birds stand together with their heads bowed and then as they begin crowing, they move to face one another raising their heads and weaving them back and forth sinuously, their open beaks to the sky, eyes firmly on each other as they renew what may be a long-held bond. The initial bonding display completed, mutual preening follows, the lovebirds obviously ecstatic to be together again. I never tired of watching the penguins renew and reinforce their breeding bonds ready for another year of rearing young, although these displays occur throughout the season, whenever the pair is reunited at the nest.

Within days the rookery was full, two birds at each nest, all of them either displaying or bickering with their neighbours. The noise was incredible, the smell unbelievable. Luckily, my supervisor and I hardly noticed it and the odour is no worse than a fishing wharf. Because krill and copepods are pigmented, the resultant guano is pink, and the rookery is denoted by its presence on the rock strata and is often several centimetres thick, mixed together with the bones of dead chicks from previous seasons. It is rather gruesome to walk over, being a testament to failed breeding and chicks that starved to death, but that is the harsh reality of nature, and every biologist must come to

Figure 46: A pair of Adélie penguins performing the mutual display at their nest site on the edge of the colony.

terms with it at some point in their working life. We conducted our first rookery-wide count of the season: a total of 4,063 adults had arrived to breed with over 1,900 pairs on their nests.

The female birds inspected the nest and often rearranged it to their liking and/or added more stones, which in their collection (stealing) caused some strife between their neighbours. Both ecstatic and mutual displays continued but now, with the female satisfied with the nest, it was time to breed.

The female lays down, either on the nest or nearby, while the male approaches from one side and hops onto her lower back. He shuffles to get balanced on his big, webbed feet and when the female lays her head back, he bends forward and vibrates his bill on hers sometimes tickling her chin and throat with his beak, his flippers stroking either side of her head and body. After a minute or two of this attention the female lifts her tail and the male twists his own down and sideways so that their cloacae connect. The sperm passes inside her, and the act is complete. He hops off, and both give their heads a good shake as though to dispel the embarrassment of what just took place.

It feels rather voyeuristic watching any animal mate. This was especially so with inexperienced male Adélies who go through the motions but forget to do the essential cloacal part. He hops off looking bemused while his mate looks around as if to say: 'Is that it?' I had seen males facing the wrong way or having been unbalanced by the female falling off, and many other hilarious sights, comical embarrassed looks all round. It was easy to laugh but we have all been there as adolescents, fumbling attempts at sex often proving very unsatisfactory. Penguins are no different, behaviours must be learnt, with attempts to breed in the early years often failing.

Adélie penguins begin returning to their natal island at two to three years of age, usually breeding for the first time between the ages of three and five. Although often unsuccessful in these early endeavours, it is all part of the learning process; success comes with age and experience. It also gives them time to develop their hunting prowess, an important factor in rearing young. With age also comes access to the better and more protected nest sites.

Mating occurs several times until with breeding over, the male penguins left Bech and a long line of them waddled and tobogganed off over the ice northwards, greatly in need of food. The male birds had not eaten in over two weeks and must now feed up ready for incubation duties.

Four or five days later the first eggs appeared. My boss and I were out monitoring the marked nests when a female stood up, a startled look on her face. And there shining brightly beneath her was a single white egg, the size of which would bring tears to anyone's eyes were

Figure 47: An Adélie penguin stands up to check its eggs and to re-arrange them in the brood pouch.

they to pass it, never mind a 70-centimetre-high penguin. The first egg is a fantastic sight and there were still many more to come. That night we cracked a bottle of wine to celebrate the first major event in the Adélie penguin breeding cycle.

Over the next few days first one and then two eggs were laid in each nest, one or two days apart. There was obvious excitement about this development throughout the rookery, the females often standing up to look at what they had produced. After a few days there were two eggs in most of the nests and the males returned from sea to incubate them. The handover was fascinating, the female both wanting to go to sea having expended a great deal of energy producing the eggs, but also not wanting to leave them. The mutual displays seemed to go on for longer, and the male now had to persuade his mate to leave the nest. The female finally moved aside, and the male shuffled forward, tucking the eggs in underneath himself where they were held against a bare patch of skin known as the brood pouch that is located low down on their abdomen. This allows the incubating bird to lie horizontal and as it does so, it shuffles its body deliciously to 'seat' the eggs in place. The female could now take the long journey over the fast ice to sea, to feed up ready for the next phase of procreation.

We conducted our second rookery-wide count: 1,933 nests contained one or two eggs, about 80% having two.

The pairs now share incubation duties, roughly 10 to 14 days for each shift (the male's first shift is usually the longer one, the female needing more time to regain weight lost due to egg production), with the other adult out at sea feeding amongst the pack ice. Incubation takes about 34 days, the first chick due to hatch in around five weeks.

The sitting bird must protect the eggs while also keeping them warm in sub-zero conditions. Marauding skuas are an issue, there being at least one pair, often two, nesting on the island and following the same breeding schedule as the penguins. These fawn and brown birds are intelligent predators. At sea they mainly eat fish, krill and carrion but with a larder on their doorstep, all they had to do was observe the incubating penguins and await their chance to strike.

Figure 48: A south polar skua in territorial display mode, wings raised, and neck arched, emitting that blood chilling laughing call.

Nests on the margins of the penguin colonies were the best targets. Inexperienced Adélies on these nests sometimes did the work for them by displacing the egg or eggs as they stood up or moved or fought with nearby adults. An egg rolling loose was an easy meal for the skuas, although first they had to grab it whilst avoiding a charging penguin, incandescent with rage. Eggs must be turned periodically to ensure that they are evenly incubated, and that is when the skuas attack, cleverly using ambush tactics, one bird harassing and distracting the standing bird, while the other swoops in and grabs an egg. It happens so fast that the penguin is left bewildered by the loss. Usually, it has a second egg to care for, and after a good body shake it returns to incubation duties, while the skuas fight over the egg yolk or embryo. The sound of skuas proclaiming territorial ownership or dominance in fights over food were a regular occurrence. With wings spread and necks arched to make themselves look bigger they let rip with gull-like hard-edged guttural 'laughing' cries, a rather chilling sound.

It may seem that skuas are a massive problem, but blizzards and their aftermath are of much greater concern, especially if a nest is in a slight dip in the rock. Incubating birds generally faced into the icy maelstrom, a nictitating membrane protecting their eyes. During blizzards, the birds were often inundated by snow, at times totally covered apart from an air hole they kept open to breathe. Humans can't stay out long in a blizzard and yet these diminutive creatures were out there at all times, their only defence being their densely packed short feathers and a layer of fat beneath. It was surprising

Figure 49: One of the 18 Bech Adélie penguin colonies, taken just before the eggs were laid. It shows the close proximity of nests, the edges being more vulnerable to skua attack.

to see how many incubating birds and their eggs came through these seemingly cataclysmic events unscathed. It is the melting ice that does the damage, without adequate drainage some eggs end up lying in an icy puddle and get chilled and die. Again, the casualties are usually the eggs of younger, more inexperienced breeders, forced into poorer nest sites. With only one clutch per year, if the eggs are thus impacted, it is game over for that season.

We could not work in blizzards and would not wish to disturb the birds in such circumstances. Other than blizzards, which were driven by cyclonic winds, our workday was governed by the katabatic or gravity wind which began in late evening, usually between 11 pm and midnight and ceased between 9 am and 10 am next day. After sunset higher density cold air flows downhill off the icecap, often travelling thousands of kilometres, and falling at least 2,000 metres in elevation to reach gale force, sometimes storm or hurricane force intensity. Mawson is infamous for this wind which is due to its location immediately below the polar plateau. To save energy the penguins hunker down in the katabatic just as they do in blizzards. Energy for breeding is limited and disturbing them in such conditions would be folly. For us to work out there would also be crazy. Once the katabatic ceased, the day was often calm and sunny, which made our work much easier and led to the birds being more amenable for study.

I had to take the katabatic wind into account during evening jaunts to the nearby islands as it was far more pleasant skiing in calm conditions. My boss had kindly agreed that if I carried a handheld radio and remained within line of sight I could ski to the islands in our immediate locality, something I was very thankful for as it fed my need for exploration and adventure. Every one of the Flat Islands was different in its shape, structure and elevation as well as access points to and from the ice. Béchervaise, Stinear and Evans Islands were the only ones with names, but I explored them all, large and small, finding snow petrel and Wilson's storm petrel nest sites and favourite places to sit quietly and reflect.

Figure 50: The Martians have landed! Bech field camp at dusk, early in the season when it became as dark as it ever did during our stay.

With the Adélie penguins now taking turns incubating eggs we had time to leave the island for station and from there to go on trips to the plateau field huts and to Auster emperor penguin rookery. Turning off the gas and power, we shouldered our packs. I sat on the rocky shore and clipped on my skis before setting off, both of us casting a long backward look at the penguins.

CHAPTER 6:

AUSTER

It was a perfect day, the sun part way up a cloudless azure sky, minus 15 degrees Centigrade: no wind. Four people donned shiny black helmets and climbed aboard four post-box red quad bikes. Engines started, we drove down through the station and onto the thick ice of Horseshoe Harbour enroute to Macey Island field hut and then Auster emperor penguin rookery 60-kilometres to the east. A dream of a lifetime was about to be realised!

The journey took us past towering ice cliffs, the continent a constant companion on our right. We drove through clusters of ice-locked islands, several with Adélie penguin rookeries and then stopped at Verner Island where I showed the others the penguin weighbridge and sensors and described how they worked. We watched the Adélies going about their business, as immediate and adorable as ever.

We drove past the mini-volcano-like Welch Island, home to the largest Adélie penguin rookery on the Mawson Coast at around 20,000 pairs. Holme Bay has 140 or so islands, Welch being the highest. The larger islands are within 10-15 kilometres of station and once they were left behind the fast ice was more open, with many ice-locked grounded icebergs and groups of small low-lying islands and rocks.

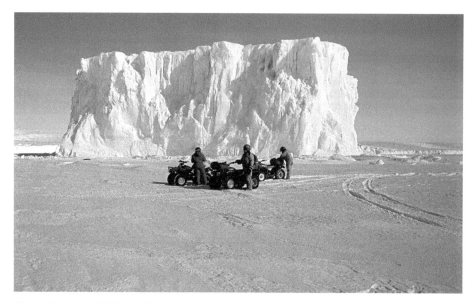

Figure 51: A smallish tabular iceberg en-route to Auster. The continental icesheet is visible in the background.

It was an ice wonderland, the likes of which I could never have imagined. Huge tabular bergs, 50-100-metres high and as large as two-or-three multi-storey office blocks, while some were like cathedrals with their own blue ice caves and grottoes. Towers and spires glistened in the sun; arches that looked so stable yet could collapse at any moment.

Many stops were made, it was impossible to drive past sights such as those. Lots of photos were taken, hands freezing quickly when taken out of warm mitts. "Quaddies thumb" was also an issue. Without heated handlebars, travelling at forty kilometres per hour, even wearing three pairs of mitts the accelerator thumb, sticking up above the frame, was exposed to the penetrating icy wind and slowly became numb.

Quad travel in Antarctica (or being out in very cold windy conditions) requires many layers of clothing beginning with woollen thermals, fleece pants and top (perhaps two of each), a one-piece freezer suit then insulated pants and jacket on top. Two pairs of thick woollen socks inside fleece lined Sorel Caribou boots keep one's feet warm. Two balaclavas and a woollen neck warmer are worn under a motorbike helmet with a polarised visor to cut out the glare. Two pairs of woollen mitts are topped off by heavy duty sledging mitts and yet still the accelerator thumb gets frost nipped.

We therefore had many excuses to stop. We revelled in surroundings that were as surreal as the imaginary

Figure 52: An example of the sort of scenes we saw en-route to Auster. Breath-taking!

world of Narnia. Looking back towards station, the coloured buildings could no longer be seen but the mountains above were in sharp relief rising out of the icecap, the ranges stretching into the distance.

We stopped at both Wiltshire Rocks and Smith Rocks where groups of Weddell seals suckled their pups next to tide cracks. We left the quads a good distance away and approached slowly and quietly on foot. The three-metre-long mothers raised their heads to observe us and then returned to repose with a deep sigh. The adults' dark brown and fawn mottled raiment shone in the sun while the pups in their pearly-grey velvet coats chewed on their flippers and turned large liquid curious eyes upon us. Sitting nearby we resisted the urge to go closer, the pups were so adorable that a cuddle would have been lovely, but that was wishful thinking. Now and then a mother called to her pup in a high-pitched bark and her offspring yipped back in childlike impression. It felt so peaceful, so calming, the atmosphere imbuing a feeling of grace.

Reluctantly we left the seals and soon the bright orange colour of Macey field hut came into view, a pleasant surprise after so much blue, white and brown. The hut, an old traverse caravan, fully insulated from the cold, was hauled here from station on skids, and it sits on a low rocky island that is also home to a small Adélie penguin rookery. It sleeps four with cooking and heating powered by gas, the bottles stored outside, while solar panels and a wind generator supply electrical power. There's an outside dunny attached to the hut and like all of the field huts and camps, all waste is taken to station for incineration.

Figure 53: A Weddell seal mother and pup basking in sunshine at minus 20 degrees. They had an access hole through the ice to the underwater world nearby.

Inside with the gas fire going, we removed our outer layers, and once the kettle boiled had mugs of strong tea that heated our innards; our hands wrapped around the mugs for warmth. We unpacked our personal gear and claimed a bunk as we were staying the night.

After lunch we climbed back on the quads and continued-on to Auster 10-kilometres further east. The emperor penguin rookery was discovered in 1957, three years after Mawson station was established, by flying officer D. Johnston who flew over it in an Auster aircraft whilst mapping the coastline. The rookery lies about 12 kilometres from the coast with approximately 10,000 pairs of emperor penguins breeding on fast ice made stable by the area's bathymetry: relatively shallow water and many grounded icebergs that lock the ice together and also provide some shelter from south easterly blizzards. The stability of this region of fast ice is crucial to the emperor penguins breeding success as the chicks must fledge before the ice breaks out during the relatively warmer summer months.

Passing the low-lying Auster Islands, the icebergs became much larger and more numerous. We decided to approach the rookery from the north through icebergs the size of small towns. Driving down the centre of a 200-metre-wide ice canyon, blue ice cliffs towered above us on either side. We were far enough away from them to be safe from an ice fall, yet close enough for the thrill of the ride. The trick was to avoid patches of deep snow, a quad bike rider's nemesis, the engine casing pushing snow ahead like a bulldozer and then grinding to a halt. We learned quickly how to extricate ourselves: we would hop off and with the machine in gear and the engine running we could usually drive it forwards out of the drift and then hop back on. On occasions when this didn't work, another rider, perhaps two would come to the rescue and help extricate the vehicle.

Even with sun visors or sunglasses the glare made it difficult to discern snow from ice but with experience one could see the snow drifts and avoid them, saving a lot of unnecessary exertion.

Figure 54: Quad bikes in part of the ice canyon near Auster. One bike with rider is almost hidden by large chunks of ice centre-left of image.

We shot out of the ice canyon into the open as though from a canon, four bikes in single file. About two kilometres ahead were the emperor penguins, loosely clustered on the ice close to more towering icebergs. We pulled up, side-by-side, in awe of the view, a vast arena of ice surrounded by icebergs, some a kilometre long. We had seen emperor penguins before, either on the pack ice from the ship, or near the station but never in such numbers. With impossibly pale blue ice cliffs shining fantastically in the sun and bluer sky above, the scene took my breath away.

We drove to within a safe distance of the rookery and dismounted, dispersing to make less of a threat, although the birds didn't seem in any way perplexed. Even before we did so there was a crowd of onlookers: non-breeding birds, known as 'mavericks', who were constantly curious had arrived to check us out. Stretching their necks this way and that, bumping into one another in their eagerness, they followed us wherever we went.

When I removed my helmet and thick balaclava the sound hit me first, the high-pitched call of the chicks, a whistle in three notes: low, high, low; and the far more complex trumpeting calls of the adults. I found the combination of sounds quite beautiful.

Figure 55: Part of Auster emperor penguin rookery. The size of the icebergs was astounding and the cold ceased to be relevant

I approached the colony low and slow and lay down on the ice. With senses wide open I took in the scene. The chicks were old enough to be left alone and were gathered in aggregations or crèches with adult birds here and there and sometimes a pair with their chick. At this stage of the breeding season both parents were coming and going to the sea over about 50 to 70 kilometres of fast ice for food, while the chicks hung out with their peers. Lines of adults were either heading away from the rookery with empty bellies or heading back towards it replete with food, the tell-tale bulge low down in their abdomens.

Up close the noise was fantastic, the chicks lifting their heads, from their fat bellies up to the sky, to call. In their pearly grey fluffy garb, the crèches looked like toddler pyjama parties, their panda-like eye patches so endearing. It seemed to me that all penguin chicks end up pear shaped, their fat bulging bellies, like little old men. There were adult emperor penguins all around me and as I sat on the ice the world's tallest penguin was at eye level with me. I lay down on my back and a single adult approached and looked down at me, its form silhouetted by the bright sky. I was being closely scrutinised and I found myself hoping that I wasn't found wanting.

Figure 56: A pair of emperor penguins have just finished the mutual display during which the chick joined in. The ice is discoloured by penguin droppings.

Adult emperors are quite simply fantastic, there are few words that can describe their magnificence and splendour: the golden orange ear patches, glowing white breast feathers (that look like densely weaved fabric) and salmon pink lower beak mandible. They were so majestic and when a pair came together and conducted the mutual bonding exercise, one was left in no doubt that their name suits them perfectly: emperor. With the chick between them, they stood facing one another, almost beak to beak. First one and then the other bowed their heads low and then trumpeted loudly, a complex sound. It has a "dee, da da dee dee, da da da" rhythm to the call, the trumpeting effected by squeezing pressurised air over the syrinx (like a human larynx but with two conduits rather than one). There was no haste, it was all done with grace and majesty.

Once the pair finished trumpeting, they raised their beaks to the sky simultaneously and then held the pose for a long moment. Then they slowly brought their heads back to the horizontal, beak to beak, face to face, it seemed in reverence and bliss. I felt a little voyeuristic witnessing the event which was played out by other pairs all across the rookery. To me it was far better than any opera, and the sound replayed years later takes me straight back to Auster.

The cacophony of the rookery was comprised of the whistling calls of thousands of chicks intermingled with the trumpeting calls of adults. The sounds rang out and echoed back off the nearby ice cliffs, blending into an emperor penguin symphony.

There was little smell due to the sub-zero conditions, but the winter's activities were writ large over the ice in dark coloured guano. Great oval olive-green and mustard-coloured smears, 50-metres in diameter decorated the ice, the result of winter huddles.

In mid-Autumn when the fast ice is well developed, and the days are growing ever shorter, long lines of adult emperors make their way from the ocean to Auster. Although rarely in exactly the same place, the rookery, comprised of several colonies, forms in the Auster vicinity. Emperor penguins do not mate for life but are serially monogamous, taking a mate each year, sometimes the same one as the previous year, and being faithful to their mate for that season.

At the colony, once both sexes are present, lone male's stand motionless with head bowed and trumpet an invitation to breed to available females who then choose a partner. The pair then come together, and the male leads his beau over the ice in an exaggerated walk which she copies. They then stop and face each other and bond via the mutual display as well as mutual preening. I would have loved to have been present at Auster at that time to hear the sound of thousands of pairs trumpeting, the calls rebounding off the ice cliffs. Mating follows soon after the pairs are established. During the bonding and mating phases, a period of a few weeks, neither sex has access to food but instead live off their fat reserves.

The single large egg is laid in May, just in time for winter, and then passed carefully to the male who does all of the 65-day incubation, during which he cannot feed. The egg is balanced on the male's black leathery feet and kept warm in a brood pouch: a bare patch of skin on the lower abdomen. A large skirt of feathered skin is then drawn down over the egg to conceal and protect it and to keep it warm. The female, having expended a great deal of energy in producing the large egg, heads off over the ice for some much-needed food. For the males with eggs, the dark months of winter are just beginning and their fast will last for a total of 120 days.

Winter blizzards can have winds of up to 200-kilometres per hour and temperatures down to minus 40-degrees centigrade. In such conditions humans would freeze to death in minutes but emperor penguins are made for this. They have densely packed feathers that are comprised of a broad flat quill about five millimetres wide and five centimetres long with fluffy down at the base and short, stiff bristly feathers along the shaft. Beneath the feathers are several layers of skin with sub-dermal fat below that. Like Adélie penguins, thermal regulation occurs through heat exchange between arteries and veins in the legs that conserve heat in the cold and release heat to the air in warm weather.

Yet even with all these amazing adaptations blizzards are problematic for male emperors because excessive heat loss burns energy and large energy losses can mean starvation and at the very least an abandoned egg as the male is forced to go to sea to feed. Every ounce of energy is needed during the long winter fast if they are to see the egg hatch and the female return.

When a blizzard begins, the male penguins, with the egg protected in their brood pouch and held on their feet, shuffle closer together. With heads down they shuffle forward into the icy blast, careful not to dislodge their precious cargo. They come together in a tight packed huddle of hundreds, sometimes thousands of birds, heads down, leaning into one another without becoming unbalanced. As the huddle gets tighter and more defined the penguins at the front, exposed to the freezing wind, peel off and shuffle around the sides to

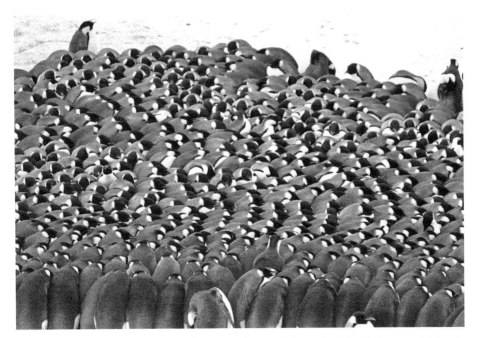

Figure 57: An emperor penguin huddle. Note how tightly packed the birds are, with heads down to conserve heat as they breathe. Credit: Australian Antarctic Division.

the sheltered rear. With this constant movement from front to rear, most birds get a long turn in the centrally protected core where the temperature may be as high as 20-25 degrees Centigrade (37.5 degrees has been recorded), a differential to the outside of 60-65 degrees. Sometimes, if a skirmish breaks out in the middle of the huddle and a gap opens a cloud of steam escapes, and it may be that it just gets too hot for the penguins who are adapted to cold and not heat.

In extreme weather the male emperors are so tightly packed that even if it were possible to be out there, and to get close enough, one could not get a flattened palm down between them. It is one of the world's great natural wonders, an evolutionary survival masterpiece. Over time the huddle creeps forward, and even with almost empty stomachs the penguins defecate, leaving the story of the huddle on the ice in their wake.

Blizzards may last a day or up to a week and the shape of dark green guano tells the story of how long the event lasted and how many birds were in the huddle. It is these large dark patches of guano that allowed researchers using satellite images to detect 11 emperor penguin rookeries around the coast of Antarctica that were previously unknown.

Once a blizzard ends the huddle breaks up into looser aggregations, at least until the next one. Some eggs are lost during blizzards, fights break out in the huddle and eggs go flying or younger less experienced birds trying to shuffle too fast, lose the egg from the brood pouch and, at minus 40-degrees, it freezes solid quickly. I saw many abandoned eggs lying around on the ice when I visited Auster. I so wished to bring one home but could not, as removing them from the continent is prohibited.

After 65 days, eggs begin hatching, a tiny beak breaking through the tough eggshell. If this occurs in calm weather the father can help his chick escape the eggshell, otherwise it must breakout by itself and it can take some time. The chick is damp from the albumen and is therefore at its most vulnerable. Protected in the brood pouch it dries and quickly develops its fluffy coat. With his stomach long empty, the father feeds the tiny chick with a milky substance produced by a gland in his oesophagus. Now the clock is ticking, if the female does not return within a few days the chick will die, and the bereaved male will head to sea.

The males look for returning females and amazingly the mothers know exactly when to return, long lines of them appearing over the ice heading back to Auster. The rookery that has been mostly silent for months suddenly erupts with trumpeting calls, the males calling to their partners to assist them in locating them, and the females calling back. On locating one another, the breeding pair seem ecstatic, the trumpeting calls reaching new levels. This mutual display is not just a bonding exercise, the chick needs to learn its parents' voices, its survival depends upon it. As the adult's trumpet, the chick makes cheeping calls to them from within the brood pouch.

Now the father must relinquish the chick that he has incubated carefully for over two months. It hatched inside his brood pouch, and he nurtured it until the female returned so he is reluctant to give it up, and things can become tense.

Figure 58: Parent birds returning to the rookery, hopefully each of them having a belly full of food for their chick.

The mother, now eager to take over the job and to provide the chick's first real meal urges him to relinquish the chick. The changeover must be quick, for if the chick is on the ice for more than a few minutes it will freeze to death. Eventually the male is persuaded to yield, and he lifts the skirt of the brood pouch, revealing the youngster to the female for the first time. With encouragement from his partner, he manoeuvres the chick off his feet and the female moves forward with her skirt raised, quickly scooping the tiny chick onto her own feet. Once in place she lowers her skirt, and the chick is once again safe in the brood pouch. When the youngster is warm again, the female once again lifts the skirt of her brood pouch, and as the chick stretches upwards, she regurgitates its first meal of partially digested fish, squid and krill, an oily concoction rich in fats.

With the transfer complete, the male who is by this time not far from starvation begins his long journey over the fast ice to the sea. He must waddle and toboggan a long way to get there and then spends around three to four weeks replenishing his fat stores and filling his belly ready for the return journey.

The adults now take turns brooding the chick, keeping it warm until it is old enough to survive in the open, while the other parent goes to sea. This period, known as the guard phase, takes about 45 days. If a blizzard occurs, the adult birds form huddles, the chicks held safely in the brood pouch. It is not easy shuffling about with a chick on their feet and, sadly, some get dislodged and freeze to death, part of the risks and spills of the huddle. Tiny frozen chicks lay on the ice and make for a pitiful sight.

While the chick is always held away from the ice on the adults' feet, on fine days the skirt of its brood pouch is pulled up and the tiny chick introduced to the world. With hundreds of adults following suit, the chicks see one another for the first time and call to one another as well as to their mums and dads.

With one parent almost always at sea and bringing back food, the chick grows quickly. It develops its own fat stores and slowly develops the ability to thermoregulate. Which is just as well as it can no longer fit in the brood pouch but must still be guarded against attack by skuas and giant petrels. It makes for a funny sight: the chicks head inside the brood pouch but its fat lower body (a big grey bum) sticking out.

If an emperor chick is not guarded by an adult, skuas and giant petrels are quick to capitalise on the opportunity for a potential meal. The skuas constantly fly overhead on the search for such possibilities, while the giant petrels roam the ice on the ground. These huge birds, the world's largest petrel: their species name says it all: *giganteus*, are an amazing sight in flight, having a two-metre wingspan, but they are ungainly on land or on the ice. Yet they are agile enough to dodge and weave around protective adult emperors in order to attack the penguin chicks and even sick adults. They

Figure 59: Emperor penguin chicks in a crèche éwith a few adult guardians. Note how many of them stand on their heels to avoid full contact with the ice. Happy feet?!

hang about on the margins of the colonies, tantalisingly close, seeming to mock the penguins. Even when these predators appear to be resting, they are just waiting their moment: a chick on its own, isolated from adult protection. The giant petrels waddle over the ice with sinister intent to further separate the chick from its parent, although now and then a chick has been abandoned. If the adult penguin is present and realises the threat, it rushes in, chest thrust out, head up and long curved beak at the ready, making the petrels back-off. Otherwise, at this early stage, when the chick does not weigh too much, it is grabbed and quickly hauled away to be killed and eaten.

When the chicks have grown sufficiently to thermoregulate they require more food and, both parents go to sea. With the threat of avian predator attack the chicks form crèches that are hundreds, sometimes thousands strong. Should a chick that has joined a crèche become isolated, the giant petrels are waiting and ready. They have chicks of their own to feed. These extremely aggressive predators work together to bring the chick down and kill it and then fight over the spoils. The crèche also has another function. Should the weather deteriorate, the chick's instinct is to huddle just like the adults. Fortunately, blizzards are less prevalent in the warmer months, but should one occur, the huddling instinct can save the chicks from freezing to death.

Our visit by quad bike to Auster was after the crèches had formed and at least half of the parents were away at sea. There was a constant stream of adult birds coming and going each way and the noise from the crèches was constant as the youngsters strove to have their voice heard and be recognised by their mum or dad who themselves trumpeted their presence. When parent and chick were reunited a chase began: with so many hungry chicks clamouring for food the adult had to shake off those not their own. Once that was achieved the chick was fed and semi-digested fish and squid could be seen as they disappeared down the hungry chick's gullet. On the fat rich diet, one could almost see them grow.

The four of us were spread out throughout the rookery, communing with the birds and taking photos. As the sun descended shadows grew longer, each 1.1 to 1.3-metre-high adult bird now had a spectre twice its height, as did we humans. The gentler light made the blue ice even bluer, and the snow was tinged slightly yellow. Our primary-coloured outer wear: bright red, yellow and green were the only strong colours to be seen and we stood out starkly against the ice and the birds.

Figure 60: The author with a retinue of curious 'maverick' emperor penguins who are always on the lookout for action. I sometimes look at this photo to remind myself that I was really there!

With arduous winter blizzards and the difficulty for younger, less experienced birds to retain the egg and/or chick on their feet, there were many casualties. This left adult emperors, who were still infused with breeding hormones with nothing to do and they caused a great deal of trouble in the breeding colonies. The maternal and paternal instinct is strong and these bereft birds, known as (the mavericks) attempted to steal other bird's chicks. The poor wee youngsters were severely jostled and trampled and sometimes died either from this treatment or they froze to death from being out of the brood pouch and on the ice for too long.

The mavericks were always on the lookout for action, and we represented just that. They were often clustered around each one of us as we sat on the ice, pushing and shoving to get a better view. They came waddling towards us in a stately line, looking so serious and majestic. Just as on the voyage to Mawson, when we were allowed onto an icefloe and a group of emperor penguins appeared, the same eagerness led to squabbles. The front bird stopped suddenly and the ones behind bumped into one another in a domino effect. Penguin slapstick broke out with loud squawks of indignation while brief flipper fights ensued. The birds that had fallen over in the melee righted themselves, shook their heads and calm was restored. They returned to their regal pose, looking at me as if to say: 'We're not usually like this you know!'

At Auster, the chicks were the stars of the show. Before me, and only a few metres away, was a host of panda faced chicks of various sizes from about 30 cm tall down to 15 cm. Amongst them, standing tall above the youngsters were a few adults. Beyond, cliffs of blue ice shimmered in the sun, while the calls of the chicks were accentuated by the echoes. I felt entranced and so happy to be there. As a child I had read about these birds and 30 years later there I was almost amongst them in their icy world, and in the place where the males had endured the harshest winter known to man. Just to be there was enough, but, when birds approached of their own free will and I was surrounded or when a small group of chicks plucked up sufficient courage to come near, I was overcome with happiness.

We stayed so long at Auster that we became ravenously hungry, and so we reluctantly left the emperors and drove back to the hut on Macey Island to be greeted by crowing Adélie penguins and the whistles of their chicks. Even Macey, 10-kilometres from Auster was paradise with huge icebergs nearby and refrozen tidal pools like mini-ice rinks amongst the pressure ridges.

With the gas heater on and food cooking we sat and drank tea, chatting excitedly about our experiences at Auster. We would return there tomorrow before heading back to Mawson. Later in bed, the heater off and the temperature falling rapidly, we all slept in thermals and fleeces. Heated huts with poor ventilation can be death traps, carbon monoxide the enemy, so rather than leave a heater on all night it was better to be a little cold.

Next day was as perfect as the last although still around minus 15-degrees. We spent a couple of hours at Auster before riding back to base, stopping to see the Weddell seals and their pups, and then climbing the peak of Welch Island. The view from the summit out over the islands and the ice topped off a marvellous trip that all of us would remember forever.

I returned to Macey field hut twice more, each time in a group of four, once in a Hägglunds and the last time on quad bikes. On both occasions we stayed overnight and visited Auster. The trips, spread a few weeks apart, allowed me to see the chicks at different stages of development. On the last journey some chicks were fledging. We were fortunate because the fast ice was melting, growing thinner with each week that passed. Indeed, not long after we returned, the station leader banned all vehicular travel on the ice, although walking and skiing were still permissible.

Figure 61: Macey field hut. The guy on the roof is clearing snow from the hut vents. Note the snow packed into the space between the small, attached store cabin and the hut caused by blizzards. The icebergs near Auster can be seen in the distance.

The last trip was unique for several reasons: the state of the ice, the opening of tide cracks at the base of icebergs at Auster, and the influx of visitors from a large tourist vessel anchored far offshore. This was the first tourist ship visit to the Mawson coast that I was aware of.

We arrived at Auster to see two large melon-shaped red and yellow tents and a helicopter parked on the ice, about a kilometre from the rookery. Brightly clad people were walking around installing marked walkways to channel the tourists, all part of their permit arrangements. It looked so incongruous after having had Auster to ourselves for months. To begin with it felt like an intrusion, especially when the large chopper ferried a total of 100 people from the ship to the improvised landing pad on the ice. We realised that we had taken ownership of Auster and the penguins and after having been trained regarding behaviour around wildlife, especially the part regarding not clustering together, it seemed ridiculous that so many people would be allowed to be there. In our defence, isolation from the world often leads to a lack of ease around strangers, and a hundred seemed like an awful lot.

But we need not have worried. The wealthy clients were only too happy to be there and conducted themselves well. They had been briefed prior to embarkation for Auster on approaching wildlife and were better behaved than some expeditioners. They also had the best camera and video technology available, long lenses requiring them to be some distance from their subjects.

It turned into a very lovely afternoon, the tourists curious about our lives in Antarctica and especially about working on a study of Adélie penguins.

It was a remarkable day, sunny with blue skies and warm: the temperature two degrees above zero. As a result, the ice was melting,

Figure 62: Exuberant emperor penguins enjoying a wash and cooling off in a saltwater pool that opened up near the base of an iceberg.

dripping from long icicles and making the ice-cliffs of the icebergs shimmer in the sunlight. There was a large tide crack near the base of one iceberg, and close to the rookery. It was open to the ocean below and the water was full of exuberant, thrashing, splashing adult emperor penguins. Having access to the sea so close to the rookery was rare and the emperors took full advantage of the treat. Once they had bathed sufficiently, they dove down, and the surface of the pool quickly became calm and glassy in appearance. I stared down into the water but could see nothing, the birds had vanished.

Others took their place and, following a good wash they too disappeared into the depths, back in the element to which they are born. Again, the pool became calm. I was standing close by with some of the tourists, wishing that I could be underwater watching them fly, when first one and then several more emperors flew high

Figure 63: This adult bird shot up out of the water and landed on the ice right before me, coated in seawater. As it stood up the film of water broke and then drained from its body like silk. I was utterly speechless.

into the air and then crashed down onto the ice like bright shining torpedoes. Dozens appeared thus, each one coated in a film of water, glistening brightly in the sunlight. We observers were all stunned. Not in a million years had I thought that I would witness an event that I had only seen on David Attenborough's nature documentaries. And yet there it was, and I wanted to shout with joy.

Many more adult birds were attracted to the slice of open water, and we had plenty of time to get photos. I envied those with videos but never thought to ask whether a copy could be sent to me on my return. Instead, I breathed it in, committing the incredible experience to memory.

With the advent of summer and higher temperatures, the expanse of fast ice was now much reduced, and the breeding adults could come and go to sea for food much more quickly. Already some chicks were bigger in both stature and girth than their parents, whose job was almost done. It was comical to see huge chicks, now with most of their adult feathers apart from some tufts on the chest and head and around the neck like a mink stole, pursuing harassed looking adults smaller than they were.

The first lot of fledging chicks had reached maximum weight, and their parents were beginning to leave, leaving their offspring to complete the process. The fledged youngsters would soon find out that they were not born to stand around on the ice, but instead for a life at sea. Soon, they would be clustered together near the edge of the remaining fast ice, afraid to dive in, often with good reason. Leopard seals lay in wait for them in the water, this event being the marine carnivores big pay cheque. Leopard seals are ferocious predators, killing and eating penguins and other seals alike. The only way for the fledgling emperors to beat the leopard seal gauntlet is by entering the sea en-masse. But nobody wants to go first, and so their departure occurs almost by default. A critical mass of fledglings builds up behind the foremost birds, pushing and shoving one another in their eagerness to approach the ice edge. Those at the front, shoved forwards, teeter and fall, and having no choice they dive in and are suddenly transformed from awkwardly waddling birds into organic torpedoes, the instinct to fly underwater fully formed. Realising an opportunity to follow the forerunners, who take the greatest risk, the rest rapidly follow. Hopefully they make it through the leopard seal danger zone unscathed.

Figure 64: A fledging emperor penguin chick that still has the remnants of its furry coat. Soon it will take to the ocean for the first time, having never seen it before.

Wishing the remaining chicks still at Auster well on their maiden voyage, we finally had to take our leave.

The journey back to Mawson was exciting. After two days when the maximum temperature remained above zero, a great deal of ice-melt had occurred. The surface of the fast ice is never uniform, there are long tide cracks where high and low tides have forced the ice upwards causing fissures that can be several kilometres long. In the colder months tide cracks are narrow, a few centimetres wide, but as the ice melts, they become wider and can be a serious hazard for quad bikes to cross. In addition, while the surface of the ice looked okay, beneath it was honeycombed and rotten. Riding over these patches the quads dropped disconcertingly, a very weird and unnerving sensation.

Fortunately, the ice beneath the rotten part was sound, although it was thinner than it had been just a few weeks beforehand: between half a metre and one metre thick instead of the two metres earlier in the season. The rotten patches looked slightly darker, and we avoided them wherever possible.

Around the islands and near ice pressure ridges, pools had developed, and the tide cracks had become enlarged. After months when Weddell seals had had to keep access holes open using their teeth, they were taking full advantage of the new development. We stopped to see mothers and pups, the youngsters now close to weaning, having grown from 25 kilos in weight to about 110 kilogrammes in six weeks. Their fluffy coats were being replaced with the darker skin of juvenile seals. Adults popped up in the tide cracks and stared at us, as surprised by our sudden appearance as we were by them. The water looked almost turquoise due to the blue of the ice, the seal's orb-like heads with long bristly whiskers, and large shining eyes made them look cat-like. They breathed loudly, looked all around and called in an almost human voice to their pups to join them in the water, some of whom were reluctant to do so. Reluctantly we moved on.

We came to a tide crack a metre wide. Could we get across or were we trapped? We rode north along it for a kilometre looking for a narrower crossing but with no success and then tried the landward side but were greeted by two-to-three-metre-high pressure ridges. We stopped and examined the tide crack and while it looked like water in the gap there was ice beneath it. With care we drove across, front wheels dropping down about ten centimetres and then up the other side. Hitting the obstacle at speed would have proven catastrophic and with no hospital for 3,000 kilometres, in Antarctica caution is far more preferable to valour.

We got back to Mawson safely having had a marvellous time. The ice melt only made the trip more memorable especially as vehicular travel over the fast ice was deemed unsafe a couple of weeks later. We had made our journey just in time and had seen the last stage of emperor penguin chick development. I wouldn't be there to see them take their first swim, but I would be thinking of them, nonetheless.

Figure 65: A seemingly never-ending tide crack that challenged our passage. They can stretch for many kilometres. Luckily, we traversed this one...with great care!

There is another emperor penguin rookery on the Mawson Coast near Taylor Bay, 90-kilometres to the west of Mawson station (in the other direction to Auster). This rookery is unusual for being on ice-free rock, the birds congregating on a small headland. This is one of two emperor penguin rookeries that do not occur on fast ice in Antarctica although the second site differs from Taylor due to the breeding birds utilising islands rather than being on the continent. There are about 3,000 breeding pairs at the Taylor rookery. Although it is on rock the adult males still carry the egg on their feet. My boss travelled there by Hägglunds to carry out the annual count of breeding birds and to resupply the hut. Sadly, there was no room in the vehicles for me, but if I had had the choice of which rookery to visit, Auster would have won hands down.

CHAPTER 7:

HENDO

Before we returned to work on Bech I had time for an overnight trip to Mount Henderson or Hendo as it is known to ANARE expeditioners. We set off one bright sunny afternoon, the four of us on quads, bombing along out of station and up past GWAMM. Myself and my three geologist companions, intent on climbing Hendo,

Figure 66: A view of Hendo from one of the Jocelyn Islands, a few kilometres northeast of station. The image provides a great perspective on the continental icesheet meeting the frozen sea of fast ice.

hopefully reaching the summit just before sunset at around 10pm. We had all been to GWAMM before, so instead we kept going with the intention of a short break on the plateau ice plain. Hendo rose up before us to our left, shining golden brown in the sun. The long western ridge of the massif known as Wave Arm leads to two peaks and we were headed beyond them. We knew that Lake Henderson lay on the other side of Wave Arm and that like all the many lakes on the plateau it was frozen solid.

Far out on the ice plain, the massif to our left, we stopped and turned off our engines. Removing our helmets, the absolute silence washed over us like a balm. It was about five pm on a beautiful Antarctic evening, the sun on its descent, yet still with a good way to go before it kissed the horizon and then rose again. Antarctic red eye caused by lack of sleep can be a real problem, especially in such spectacular surroundings, the urge to stay up all night to watch almost perpetual sunsets was often hard to resist. Being with this group I knew that we might at least remain up well after midnight and indeed the plan was to do just that, to be on top of Hendo for the witching hour.

We sat on our bikes, the engines ticking as they cooled and looked around across the vast rolling blue-ice plain at the mass of the North Masson's and the long-jagged line of the David Range. The splendour of the Antarctic plateau never failed to fill me with wonder.

Reluctantly we started our machines and rode parallel to the long western flank of the massif. Once past the two towering peaks we did a wide arc around the most southern one and stopped briefly to survey the next section. Before us was a long, wide snow-covered ice slope set at an incline of about 20-degrees, angled even more sharply upwards in some places. It looked easy but we knew it could pose a challenge if one strayed off the main route. Thick snow lay in wait for the uninitiated and even on the main route constant motion was required in order to maintain traction; stopping the quad could lead to being bogged down in drifts. It was a great ride that took us up into the broad saddle between the main peak of Hendo and the southern outlying crag. Beyond that to the south lay Fischer Nunatak and the great East Antarctic icesheet. We contoured around a rocky outcrop and rode over a large snow-covered ice tongue before traversing rocky ground to reach Mawson's highest field hut. The hut is beautifully perched on the northern side of a low ridge, protected from the worst of the south-easterly winds. Through its picture window one looks northwards through the gap between two peaks, one of which is Hendo and out over Wave Arm and Lake Henderson far below. In the distance the terminus of the icesheet curves out of sight with brown islands amidst the fast ice beyond that stretches to the distant horizon. The hut has a wide wooden deck on its northern (sheltered) side with a long bench to sit on so that one could soak up the view.

Figure 67: Hendo hut (red) can be seen just below the ridgeline at centre with Fischer Nunatak beyond amidst the icesheet of the polar plateau.

Like most of the other field huts at Mawson, Hendo sleeps four and has an outside dunny. We unloaded our packs and secured the quads nearby in case a blizzard or the katabatic buried them in snow. We decided to have dinner and then head off to climb Hendo, but a hot cuppa came first, the four of us lined up on the bench outside in the sunshine, laughing and joking, easy banter.

We had brought our dinner from station; freshly made chicken tikka masala with fried rice and some leftover apple pie for dessert, tinned custard too. We took our time, there was no rush, there was no darkness to contend with.

Then with daypacks containing emergency gear and an extra layer of clothing we tramped over a blizzard tail, snow over ice, onto rock strewn ground and then onto a steep rocky scree slope. Climbing the

Figure 68: The view north from Hendo's summit with glacial flow lines in the icesheet as it approaches the coast. The flat zone beyond is the frozen ocean (fast ice) with Bech being the largest island at centre.

scree made my lungs burn with the cold but it was an easy enough gradient, especially as we were all mountain enthusiasts and had done ridge-line traverses either in Tasmania or in Victoria. I love rock hopping and scrambling and the careful placing of feet to avoid sliding backwards, climbing in time with one's breathing. Slow and steady with constant upward momentum works well for me. Then came huge, tilted rock slabs that for some would require ropes but, with great hand and foot holds on dry granite, it was a pleasure to scramble up them, if a little unnerving when looking down between my legs.

On cresting the summit, the view opened before us as though a huge curtain had lifted. It was an amazing surprise, the likes of which I had only experienced when climbing Pindars Peak close to Tasmania's south coast. On summiting Pindars Peak a large swathe of the south

Figure 69: The author and a friend, each with a wide grin, on Hendo's summit. It's cold but the views are out of this world!

coast opens before you, the shoreline etched by long white sandy beaches and the great Southern Ocean spread out as far as the eye can see, dotted with islands. The surprise is compounded by the sound of the surf which rolls up the peak's southern slopes on the breeze. Here in stark contrast to the view from Pindars Peak, the ocean was frozen and dotted not just with rocky islands but with icebergs too. Immediately below us was Lake Henderson, a huge ice lake embraced by arms of rock, Wave Arm on one side and much larger Goldsworthy Ridge on the other. Beyond it were great rivers of ice flowing inexorably towards the coast, the flow lines clearly visible. Only from the summit of Hendo did I see those enormous rivers of ice so well defined, and I understood much more about the plasticity of ice, and that while blue ice is harder than concrete it also flows almost like its liquid counterpart, although it takes thousands of years rather than hours to reach the sea.

The sun was setting, and the scene was bathed in fiery gold and crimson, the rocks below and around us sun-kissed golden orange. We four, muffled in warm clothing, clustered on the summit in complete silence, drinking it all in, struck dumb by the scene's magnificence. We were joined by a flock of snow petrels that swooped and swirled all around us, like a dozen large white handkerchiefs thrown into the air.

The four mountain ranges stitched in neat lines from east to west across the ice glowed in glorious sunlight, while to the south the great white yonder stretched away into the unknown. Part of me wanted to be out there with nothing but ice in every direction, while another part, driven by ego, feared homogenous white oblivion and that out there I might cease to exist. I could not comprehend what it would be like to man-haul a sledge all the way to the pole and having experienced blizzards close to a safe haven, how much energy and courage it must take to keep going, and the suffering involved in that endeavour. Hauling day after day over a white wasteland, often with no obvious horizon, aware only of the snow-covered ground at one's feet. The hard truth is that humans are not meant to be here, and the small toehold we have on the edge of this vast continent is a reminder of our frailty in the face of a hostile environment and climate. And yet the icecap, that great white desert still tugged at my sleeve.

Having lain on Hendo's summit for an hour, the sun long gone, cold and cramp were setting in, and we had to make a move. A stiff breeze had sprung up, possibly the start of the Katabatic or just the result of altitude and it was freezing. The scramble down the rock slabs warmed us and after crossing the scree and the ice tongue we reached the hut that was still a little warm from our recent occupation. After a cup of tea and some cake we clambered into our sleeping bags, rugged up ready for the hut cooling down to well below zero overnight. Luckily there were no heavy snorers, and, after thanking my stars for sharing Hendo's summit splendours with these fine people, I drifted into happy oblivion.

Next day we had a lazy breakfast and then clambered up Hendo's western summit to get a different perspective on the Hendo massif as well as Fisher Nunatak, the other mountain ranges and the icy interior. The sun was high in the sky, the glare at its peak. The view was stupendous. We stayed as long as we could, but the cold always wins.

After lunch we packed up and had fun descending the long snow slope on our quad bikes, back to the rolling blue ice plateau. Re-joining the drum line we followed it along Wave Arm, its rocky spur 100-metres or more above us. Then leaving the marked trail we rode around the northern end of the arm and into the mouth of Lake Henderson, the ice lake that we had seen from Hendo's summit. The lake is about three kilometres long and half a kilometre or so wide and is probably the result of a retreating glacier whose surface has melted and refrozen many times. Features in Antarctica that look almost new can be ancient, but it sure made for great fun on a quad bike, as the surface was glassy and there were no snow drifts to cause the bikes to tip over. We did donuts until we were dizzy and then great sliding sideways skids turning through 180-degrees to face the opposite direction. We then did the latter move in a line, working on our timing until it became a quad bike dance on ice. We forgot about climate change as we whirled and curled the machines, sending them sliding for 40-50-metres across ice as smooth as glass.

Figure 70: Lake Henderson with the long promontory of Wave Arm viewed from the slopes of Hendo. Wave Arm is in shadow while Goldsworthy Ridge, that leads from Hendo on its eastern side is lit up by the sun.

After 15 minutes of fun, we rode to the lake's southern end where there were rocks scattered over the ice, having fallen from above, who knew how long ago. Pulling up we switched off the engines and removed our helmets. The silence quickly enveloped us, even more so because we had been riding noisy growling motorbikes. With boot chains attached for walking on the slick surface, the four of us split up and went our separate ways. Sitting on a rock near the shore I was once again enraptured by the profound silence. The great rock arms embraced the ice lake while the distant opening to the north made me feel as though I was in the gullet of some mythical creature. We remained alone for close to an hour, each of us in need of solitude before returning to station.

The cold finally drove us to action, and we did some rock scrambling to warm ourselves up. Then we boarded our metal steeds and set off on the journey back to Mawson. Our adventure had been the best way possible to share time together, and we all felt thankful to Hendo and the icecap for more experiences that we would never forget. I later lost touch with my excellent companions, but they still reside in my memories, as only good friends can.

We stopped off at GWAMM on the return journey and clambered onto the traverse trailers, checking out the living quarters and the kitchen van, all clean and ready for the next traverse. Sitting on a veranda outside we looked out over the islands, icebergs and fast ice. I could see my field camp home on Bech and anticipated returning to the penguins and snow petrels to continue my work and to travel once again to the icebergs to sit with the Weddell seal mothers and their pups.

I told them that the name or acronym GWAMM was comprised of the Christian names of four women probably born in the 1940s or 1950s and we had fun coming up with some suggestions like Gloria, Winifred, Amy, Martha and Marilyn.

From GWAMM it was a short leg back to station, arriving in time for a blissful hot shower before Saturday night dinner, always a special affair accompanied by wine to mark the weekend. I would still have Sunday to get prepared for heading back to Bech and developing more slides.

CHAPTER 8:

ICEBERG FORAY

Living on Bech there was plenty of time outside of work hours to explore, both on Bech and via skiing to the nearby islands. But having fully explored the islands I was eager for new horizons. There were two icebergs about three kilometres away, both as big as half a dozen city blocks. I had had my eye on them since we first arrived and now, I could resist their lure no longer.

Figure 71: Skiing towards one of my favourite icebergs on a beautiful calm evening, temperature: minus 18 degrees.

When we first arrived on Bech in mid-October the sun set for only a couple of hours each day, with the intervening twilight, bright enough for walking or skiing.

In the evenings, after dinner, my supervisor was usually ensconced in front of her laptop in the camp office entering data from her field notebook and uploading and sorting data from the weighbridge. I knew from experience that she would be there for at least two to three hours. She had never called me on the handheld radio during my evening excursions to the nearby islands, merely keeping a listening watch in case I called her. That was perfect for me: taking proper care, I was free to roam, so long as I remained in line of sight for radio communications.

It was always a wonder to me clipping on my skis and leaving the island, heading out into the world's greatest wilderness. The fast ice is a super-highway that can take you hundreds of kilometres. Boats are all well and good but two-metre-thick ice allows you to go almost anywhere.

The main hazard I had to be aware of was the katabatic wind that generally kicked in about midnight and then blew fiercely until 10 am the next day. Skiing back with the katabatic blowing in one's face would be difficult and could, in reduced visibility lead to getting lost and or hypothermia and even death. I had to leave the icebergs at 11 pm at the latest to be safe.

On this occasion, only two weeks after we arrived on Bech, I left the island just as the sun was setting in a blaze of glory, the tissue thin cirrus clouds forming a slowly changing canvas of crimson and gold. The light was evening gentle, the icebergs highlighted in pastel blues and pinks. The only sound was the shoosh of my skis and the panting rush of my breath. At minus 22 degrees and humidity in the negative, the air was far too dry for my breath to condense, instead turning directly to ice in my short beard. Skiing was warm work, so I skied just in my freezer suit with insulated pants over the top but without the added jacket on top.

With regular gale force and storm force winds the surface of the fast ice was a mixture of snow patches and drifts with large areas of blue ice where the wind had scoured it clean. There were also areas of sastrugi where the surface ice was channelled, ridged and corrugated. Skiing was therefore a mixture of straightforward arm pumping, shoulder width ski-sliding, classic style on the snow patches and skating over the stretches of blue ice, pushing off with my poles, my skis in a 'V' shape. Skiing over sastrugi was bone jarring and best avoided. The diversity of styles employed was invigorating for me; there was no boredom from tedium whilst on the ice.

Figure 72: Weddell seals near the base of the iceberg. Note the rounded lower ledges where wave action has smoothed the ice when the icebergs have been surrounded by ocean.

My destination icebergs had been there for several years, grounded on a rocky shoal about 100-200-metres below. The bergs had no doubt come from the terminal face of the nearby Forbes Glacier, breaking free or calving during the late summer when the ocean was largely ice-free. Then years of being surrounded by ice and then subjected to big swells (once the fast ice broke out) had left their mark. Large, rounded ledges 10-20 metres high and deep were topped by crumbling 70-metre-high ice cliffs. The ice at the top of the cliffs was deeply fissured through decay, enormous towers and blocks of ice leant together like trios of drunken men. On the northern side of the left-hand berg was a perfect spire that would have looked good on a medieval castle. They were imposing structures, each the size of half a dozen city blocks, several storeys high. Around their base lay scattered chunks of ice that ranged in size from a washing machine to a Landcruiser. There was no doubt where they had come from.

And yet a dozen female Weddell seals lay within the kill zone, each with a pearly grey pup. The reason for this proximity was the tide cracks that are prevalent around icebergs and islands. The seals use their teeth to keep the access holes open, spinning upright inside the hole, their upper canines and incisors doing the work. The ridges all around the hole's rim told the story. The seals must maintain the holes, ensuring they remain large enough for access and clearing any new ice that forms overnight.

Skiing out there I felt as free as a bird. I loved Bech but it was made so much better by my trips away, solitude does that for me. I always returned refreshed, and during 24-hour daylight the exercise also helped me to sleep. Returning to Bech by midnight still gave me eight- or nine-hours rest, ready for work next day when the katabatic wind eased.

As I travelled north the icebergs grew steadily until they dominated my field of vision, and I could see a dozen brown sausage shapes near their base. The seals heard me coming a kilometre out, with one ear close to the ice the sound of my skis would have been like having one's ear to a rail line listening to the approach of a distant train. I stopped 50-metres away and unclipping my skis attached some ice chains to my boots to make walking on slick ice safer. Approaching slowly, I reduced my height in a crouch and sat down about 15-metres away. A couple of heads were raised, the mothers checking me out but having done so they lay back down and slept.

Figure 73: A Weddell seal mother and pup. Like most baby mammals their own limbs or appendages are constantly fascinating.

Those were such peaceful times, sitting with the seals as they slumbered, their pups either suckling or lazily rolling over to gaze in my direction, looking at me with large liquid eyes. Like any baby they seemed surprised by their appendages, often chewing on their fore-flippers or waving them around as though they had just discovered them. The only sounds were the odd snoring seal, the sound of wet farts (not mine) and sudden intakes of breath. Even hauled out on the ice seals only breathe when required. Otherwise, the silence was absolute. I could hear the rush of blood in my ears and would have stopped both my heart and my breathing if I could just to hear what the silence was like without my autonomic functions. On Bech the thump, thump, thump of the station generators was sometimes blown to us on the wind. Out by the icebergs there was no other human sound, and I treasured the experience. These were moments that would never be repeated, and I soaked them up as best I could.

With the icebergs towering over me and the beautiful grey and brown mottled seals with their grey velvety pups nearby, the sun was setting in a blaze of glory that lasted an hour, the sky wreathed in golden yellow and crimson with the tops of the icebergs tinted pink. If I looked behind me over the vast plain of ice to the chocolate-coloured islands and beyond to gleaming ice cliffs and the icecap, I could see mountain ranges golden brown in the sun. In moments like those I felt as though I was a part of that place and accepted by its native inhabitants. It was a different world, it felt like an alternate universe.

Figure 74: The icebergs themselves were fascinating and I circumnavigated them on each visit to look at all their features.

One night in particular sticks in my mind. I was sitting quietly with the Weddell seal mothers and pups, soaking up the experience and storing it away for when I was elsewhere, perhaps on a city bus or stuck in traffic. Other worldly sounds suddenly filled the air around me. Startled, I looked all around but there was nothing there that they could have come from, the nearby seals slumbering on.

There were long descending trills, warbles, whistles and pings. The trills began high in an alto and then descended slowly through the range to a baritone before finishing on several long-drawn-out staccato clicks that dropped into a bass and then beyond my hearing range. The sounds felt as if they came from within me, as though I was the instrument while the source was unknown. I thought that only whale song could have that effect. I finally twigged that these sounds were bull Weddell seals calling from beneath the ice, holding territory and singing for the females who on weaning their pups would again come into season. I tried to imagine them twisting and turning in their favoured element right below me or just hanging in the water column as they sang. Who knows how many there were, by the songs I thought probably three or four, although there could have been younger bulls there too, developing their repertoire. I wondered whether the song had evolved in order to encourage the females into oestrus, it seemed a reasonable idea. Whatever, I was transfixed, they were sounds I had never heard before, they were like some alien song, but one that entered my soul and permanently lodged there.

It lasted for 40-minutes or so before ending as suddenly as it had started. I heard a couple of individuals surfacing in one of the nearby

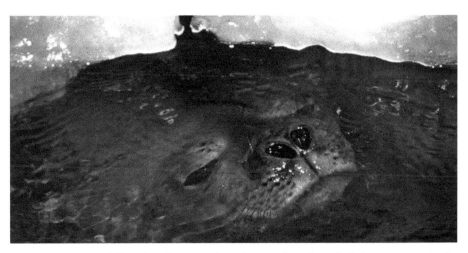

Figure 75: A Weddell seal surfacing to breathe in a breathing hole kept open using its teeth. I often heard the pneumatic hiss as they sucked in air at a nearby ice-hole without actually seeing them.

breathing holes to inhale deeply, no doubt having sung themselves breathless.

It was that same evening that I stayed too long, having been entranced by the songs and completely lost to the tyranny of time. I had already been there for two hours prior to the seals singing: an hour spent skiing around and between the icebergs and another hour sitting quietly with the mothers and pups. It was now 11.30pm and a light south easterly breeze had just begun. The katabatic had started, cold air falling downwards off the icecap and picking up speed with every kilometre travelled.

I carefully retreated from the seals and clipping into my skis set off at a brisk pace. Within 15 minutes the light breeze grew to a 20-knot wind and continued rising to gale force, spindrift blowing all around my legs. I felt panic rising and attempted to ski straight, the faster to get back to the safety of Bech. But on blue ice I was being blown backwards, no matter how hard I skied, and I fell several times, cursing the wind. I felt the adrenalin kick in, fight or flight in full flow. I knew that out there, in blizzard conditions, panic could kill, and I stopped and took some deep breaths, closing my eyes and getting my head together. Rationally I knew that it was unlikely that I would die out there. With gaps in visibility, I could always glimpse the islands. It would take me longer, but if I skied only on the snow patches and drifts, I would get safely home. Even if I had to remove my skis, I could crawl there keeping my body mass low, creating less of an obstacle to the wind.

By dodging from snow patch to snow patch I kept underway although it was grievous hard work. The wind was buffeting and bullying me, my lower half lost in spindrift. Luckily, I always carried emergency gear including ski goggles. Without them I might have perished, sunglasses no match for the icy maelstrom, and without sight one is lost. Sweating with exertion and fear I pushed on although I was far more worried about being found out as a fool, and my evening excursions banned than anything else. Every metre was hard won but I got there. Reaching the dry rock of Bech was a great release and I took several deep breaths to slow my racing heart. I unclipped my skis and crept to the store shed where I kept them and also divested myself of snow and ice before entering the warmth of the living pod. My boss was sitting near the stove reading and barely looked up, asking whether I had been up at the southern end of the island as she knew of my predilection for wild weather. I mumbled something in reply, and she went back to her book.

I never told anyone about my near miss, but I was never late leaving the icebergs again. I skied out to the icebergs several times during my stay, only ceasing my excursions when the ice became unsafe. The freedom that the fast ice provided was intoxicating, there were so many possibilities for exploring islands and icebergs and I had the ice wonderland all to myself. I was not meant to go out there alone, but I had a feeling that I would never be back, and I knew that I would

Figure 76: A Weddell seal slumbering on the ice. Isn't life grand!

regret not pushing the boundaries of possibility. All these years later I am so glad that I took that decision. I'm sure that as is always the case, there are those who will judge me for breaking the rules and call me reckless and selfish but there will be many others who will applaud my endeavours. Life is for living and experiences like that are rare as well as priceless and eternal.

CHAPTER 9:

BLIZZARD

Another fascination for me in Antarctica was blizzards. The sheer power of the wind, a blinding white maelstrom, often with zero visibility, and the potential for disaster. I loved them in short instalments; too much and I froze but a little was exciting. Of course, doing so while remaining safe was paramount. In Antarctica, nature's elements are unleashed like the hounds of inverted hell. The world is obscured by wind driven snow and ice, the wind so strong that anything out on the fast ice is blown all the way to open water, far to the north.

In Antarctica, blizzards are far more common in winter when deep cyclonic low-pressure systems whirl almost unceasingly around the continent. These are the same systems, at least their northern extensions, that batter the western shores of Tasmania. Mawson in spring still experiences about ten blizzard days each year, there being very few if any during summer.

A blizzard is defined as being a storm with large amounts of airborne snow and ice, winds greater than 34 knots (63 kilometres per hour) and visibility less than 100 metres for a period of an hour or more. The temperature must be sub-zero.

Figure 77: A blizzard on Bech. The Adélies are hunkered down protecting their eggs from the icy blast. The hazy apparition of the office pod can just be seen in the background.

During my stay at Mawson, we had roughly 11 days of blizzard conditions. I was on station for four of them (one blizzard lasted two days), on the plateau for one and on Bech for the rest. While I ventured outside during the blizzards on station, I had to have a good reason for doing so. On Bech, so long as I remained safe I could do as I pleased.

I left the field camp fully rugged up for quad bike travel, looking a little like a canary-yellow Michelin man. Better to be too warm than too cold. A good pair of goggles was essential during blizzards, otherwise one could not see.

I passed the incubating Adélies, hunkered down against the icy blast. At least I had the choice of being out in such conditions. The brooding penguins had no such choice, although they did have the advantage over me of feathers that could not be breached by the strongest wind, thick skin and a layer of fat underneath. Already snow had accumulated around them and on them and it was increasing with every passing minute. I wondered what they might look like when I returned.

I battled on past the rookery, avoiding the exposed summit ridge and keeping to lower ground. There are many rocks and boulders scattered around Bech, left behind by the retreating ice sheet 10-15 thousand-years ago. They made excellent anchor points and sheltered me for fleeting moments in my advance southwards.

Figure 78: Can you imagine wind driven snow and ice howling down off the icecap and across the expanse of fast ice to blast me in the face at Bech's southern end? Photos taken in the maelstrom on the day proved to be an inscrutable white void because the visibility changed so rapidly.

The wind punched and buffeted me but so long as I dodged between the rocks, I was able to make headway steadily trudging towards the southern end of the island. It was an arduous journey but thrilling too. Something within me needs these extreme conditions from time to time to blow away the cobwebs and to ground me. In the same way, I love being out in thunderstorms or by a river or waterfall in flood. The sheer power that the earth's atmosphere can unleash, and its consequences invigorate me in a way that nothing else can. Knowing that there is a warm refuge, be it house, car or in this case a space age pod allows me the experience without fearing for my life.

It was excellent fun, like a military campaign, fighting the odds to creep up on the enemy, from boulder to boulder I dodged all the way to the islands southern end. Once there I found a large rock to hide behind. Then with my body protected I lifted my head and stared into the vortex, ice and snow blown thousands of kilometres down off the Antarctic icecap and hurled out over the ice. It seemed to come from a central point, somewhere ahead of me but that was an illusion. It was like my experience on the ship's bridge at night-time when windblown snow was transformed into mesmerising silver cables by the searchlights. As on that occasion it was transcendental in its effect and although this time, I was outside, battered by powerful winds it was as though I was on a motorbike travelling at 120-kilometres per hour. I felt utterly invigorated but also at peace. It was just me and the elements; exactly as I like it. I would have dearly loved to share it with someone who appreciated the experience as much as I did but there was nobody there but me.

Visibility varied between zero and 20 to 30-kilometres, although the latter periods were rare. When it did clear I could briefly see the primary colours of the station buildings and even the hazy brown of mountain ranges high on the plateau. The curtain lifted occasionally by varying degrees and then was rapidly drawn back down, once again obliterating the world all around me and cocooning me in a howling vortex of snow and ice. The battering winds rose and fell in velocity, the gusts far more brutal as I discovered when I lifted my head: it felt like riding pillion on a motorbike at ridiculously high speed, my head was rocked backwards by the force.

An hour out there was enough, the chill became telling, especially around my goggles and even my well protected hands. That for me was part of the thrill: understanding just how hostile this place could be, how inhospitable it is to humans. And yet behind me at the islands other end the Adélie penguins might spend days exposed to these atrocious conditions. Their commitment to breeding is absolute and to me their sheer tenacity is legendary.

The challenge on my way back to camp was not to be pushed and shoved by the wind so that I ended up galloping, reaching terminal velocity, my body outpacing my feet to be thrown sprawling onto the ground or worse, crashing into a boulder. I had to use the obstacles in the opposite way to my journey southwards, using them to break my headlong rush and to hide behind in order to get my breath back. Storms, especially blizzards, literally take one's breath way and make it very hard to breathe.

I had been away for an hour and the incubating penguins were now almost inundated by snow. In another hour they would be covered, the birds maintaining an opening around their heads in order to breathe. Even from the rookery the camp appeared and disappeared in the blizzard, the weird looking hazy shapes of the pods making it look like an alien world.

On returning to the living pod, I took great care with the door which could with poor handling be ripped off its hinges and hurled out to sea. It would not have made me popular. Inside I hung up my gear and thawed out before the welcome gas fire while the kettle boiled for tea and slices of home-made bread toasted under the grill.

CHAPTER 10:

SNOW PETRELS

I had another job on Bech. My boss was responsible for data entry on the penguin project and spent long hours in the late afternoons and evenings transferring data from her field notebooks, and from the two weighbridges (one on Bech, the other on Verner Island), together with writing daily reports on our work. It was a task that I would have found arduous, but she seemed to enjoy it, and it freed me to conduct the snow petrel project, that had been carried out annually for some years.

These incredible birds, about the size of a racing pigeon, live amongst the pack ice for most of the year, feeding on fish, squid, krill and

Figure 79: A snow petrel inside its nest cavity. This pair were lucky that their nest was not totally inundated during the blizzard.

copepods, which they snatch from the surface waters. They are often seen roosting, sometimes in large numbers on icebergs, although being snow-white they are difficult to spot. If disturbed, for example by a large orange ship, they explode into the air as though someone has cast a ream of white A4 paper from the top of the iceberg.

Like most Antarctic seabirds, snow petrels require ice-free rock in order to breed and do so mostly in small colonies of 50-200 birds although some colonies number over a thousand. Their preferred nest sites are single entrance rock cavities, tiny caves, just big enough for an adult, and when the time comes for a growing chick. The cavities, usually under ledges, boulders or rock-slab overhangs, must be defendable against skuas and have either a flat bowl like depression or be only slightly sloping, to prevent the single egg from rolling away. In addition, the aspect of the nest cavity is important. The prevailing winds during blizzards and the katabatic can inundate nests with ice and snow, causing failure, so sites that look north are preferred. There are roughly 200 potential nest sites with varying aspects on Bech, but in order to monitor occupancy etc the researcher has to be able to see inside the cavity. Thus, the study group was confined to 50 marked nests.

The islands of Holme Bay and the summits of peaks and nunataks in the Framne Mountains are home to many snow petrel colonies but they also breed much further inland. For instance, there is a large breeding colony in the Prince Charles Mountains of MacRobertson Land (of which the Mawson Coast is part), a distance of 540 kilometres in a direct line from Mawson but 440 kilometres from the coast.

Nesting occurs between November and March although birds may be present on the island all year-round. Gravel or small stones (or even bare rock) comprise the nest into which they lay a single white egg between late November and mid-December.

Snow petrels mate for life and return to their birth site to breed. Being relatively long-lived the same nest cavity may be used year after year (known as site fidelity), especially if it meets their exacting demands. The Bech snow petrel study capitalised on this knowledge; the marked nests usually being occupied every year.

When on Bech I monitored the marked nests daily, checking for occupancy, or the presence of an egg or a chick in each nest. Chicks begin hatching in mid-January, with hatchings occurring until late-February. We were due to leave Bech in early February so I would not be present to record them all. Fledging occurs between the end of February and the third week of March, after which the juveniles take their first flight and join their parents out amongst the pack ice.

Snow inundation caused by katabatic winds and blizzards is the greatest cause of snow petrel nest failures, often with roughly 50% of nests being abandoned as a result. Thus, their success is highly weather dependent, with some years worse than others.

Every day when we were on the island, I would visit the nests marked by a numbered plastic marker screwed into the rock close by the nest site. It took me time to gain the bird's trust and I made sure that I never startled them, this being their most important life event. Their defence mechanism when threatened is comparable to that of fulmars: projectile vomit, the bright pink foul-smelling oil created by the partially digested prey of copepods and krill is impossible to wash off, the clothing item in question sometimes having to be trashed. They vomit on each other too while tussling over a mate or a nest site, some birds splashed in pink, the feathers no longer waterproof. It is highly effective against skuas, and few eggs or chicks are taken by them as a result.

Without being intrusive, and to avoid being vomited upon (fortunately it never happened, or at least it never hit me), I monitored nest occupation and attendance carefully, often lying flat on nearby rock-slabs and using binoculars.

Monitoring the snow petrels was not a job, more a delight. It allowed me to commune a little with these special birds that are found nowhere else on the planet. From inside their burrows, they regarded me warily but soon became familiar with my presence and so relaxed. I have always spoken to animals be it domestic or wild mammals and of course birds. I tell them I mean no harm and I avoid direct eye contact, just sitting quietly nearby. Birds and animals appear to understand my intent and do not flee. The snow petrels watched me calmly as I wrote down my observations in my field notebook. I gave them more distance when they were incubating the egg to avoid them flying from the nest and the egg becoming chilled.

Occupancy of the study nests was high, 46 out of 50 and I recorded 43 of them with an egg. Sadly, several nests were inundated by

Figure 80: Snow petrels having a brief rest. The rear bird is marked with pink vomit, probably acquired during a tussle over a nest site.

snow as a result of katabatic winds and blizzards, some nest cavity entrances being completely blocked. But the rest, 29 or so nests with an egg, survived and although I recorded only 18 chicks before leaving Bech, I had high hopes for the rest. I never saw skuas attacking the nests, and as a result recorded no losses to them. The small nest cavities and the threat of projectile vomit and non-waterproof feathers works!

From the snow petrel nests I climbed the remaining way to the islands summit. It was a great spot with airy 360-degree views. Even at 47 metres elevation it towers over the nearby Flat Islands and provides superb views of the station and icecap and out to the ice locked icebergs. There were nearly always snow petrels in the air all around me, swooping and diving, carving the air, intermingling with the others and then breaking apart. They were rarely still, landing briefly in small groups on the sloping slabs of rock before once again taking to the air. As most photographers know, capturing images of birds in flight is challenging and so I soon gave up and just enjoyed watching them.

The summit also turned out to be an open-air gym. A previous volunteer had left two five-kilogram dumbbells up there and I made full use of them. What a place to keep fit and with views to die for.

On my way back to camp, pumped from being with the snow petrels and then doing my exercises, I always went via my favourite rock, shaped like a giant turtle, neck outstretched, it even had a dimple for an eye and a crevice for a mouth. Naturally, I named it turtle rock and I often sat on its neck to survey my domain. Me and that rock were pals and I spoke to it too. Mad I know but nobody was there to comment on my strange behaviour.

Figure 81: Giving turtle rock some loving. He or she always looked rather glum, perhaps due to my inane chatter!

My walking route to the snow petrels changed one day when I heard the frightening whoosh and rush of air within a few centimetres of my head. Skuas take no prisoners when guarding their eggs or chicks and are not averse to striking one on the head. With my hands above my head, I bid a hasty, hunch-backed retreat. The skuas, satisfied now by the distance between me and the nest, landed nearby and performed their territorial display; wings high above their heads, necks arched, heads down, screaming at maximum volume. A long strung-out guttural laughing call that says: this is mine, stay away, bugger off! I buggered off and forthwith was wary of entering their territory.

CHAPTER 11:

BECH: HATCHLINGS

It was early December on Bech, and the Adélie penguins were well into their second incubation shift. The skuas had taken some eggs, and others had been chilled and made non-viable by meltwater following blizzards. Most of the birds were still sitting tight, every now and then getting up to rearrange or turn the eggs or to change places with their mate.

There was sufficient work to keep us engaged until the eggs hatched which would herald our busiest time. One breeding adult would then be at sea feeding, while the other incubated and guarded the chick or chicks. We prepared the equipment for this period, testing the electronic devices: satellite trackers and time-depth recorders (TDR's), and checking the penguin capture, and processing gear as well as the lavage (stomach flushing) equipment. We had cans of spray paint for marking the birds that would carry the devices or that had been subject to lavage. The latter is not a pleasant process, the penguin is captured and held upside down while its stomach is flushed into a fine meshed sieve in order to obtain the contents which are then assessed to determine what it has eaten and how much. A necessary evil as far as penguin researchers are concerned but not a pleasant job and certainly unpleasant for the penguin who then has to return to sea for more food. Marking them ensured that they would not be selected for the process again.

Meanwhile, inside each fertilised egg beneath the sitting birds, new life had developed, the embryo having grown incrementally from a bundle of divided cells into a tiny being that resembled a bird. Soon now, the chicks would be fully formed, heads and legs incongruously large, bluish bulging eyes sealed shut. The incubating birds were religious in turning and tending the eggs to ensure that they were evenly incubated.

Sadly, there are always some eggs that are infertile and yet others that are abandoned for reason or reasons unknown, perhaps a breakdown in the pair bond with one bird failing to take proper care of the eggs. Unattended eggs soon freeze or are taken by skuas.

By the second week of December, we were watching closely for the tell-tale signs of hatching: incubating birds fidgeting on the nest or standing up more regularly. This was an event that we did not want to miss: the first chick to hatch, at least on our 200 study nests. Seeing the newly hatched chicks of any species is special, for me it is a breath-taking moment. Such vulnerable new life, blind and often pink and hairless, wobbling about, trying to lift their heads for the first time. But because I was so invested in the Adélies, both working with them and then sitting with them in the evenings after work, the time of hatching was ripe with anticipation. There was also a frisson in the air amongst the birds; they knew better than we did when the event would occur.

Then, a few days later, we were observing our study nests when a bird stood up, and there, beneath it one egg had a small hole in the side with a tiny black beak protruding. This splendid vision lasted 10-15 seconds and then the parent bird lay back down again. The next time the penguin rose, the egg was split transversely, the albumin wet chick curled up inside. On the following occasion the chick was free of the eggshell and was attempting to struggle upright. It was a marvellous sight and one I will always remember.

That night we celebrated the first penguin chick with a bottle of wine, a rare occurrence on Bech. New life was upon us and with the chicks hatching we knew that our busiest time was imminent.

Figure 82: The moment of hatching. The chick's eyes will open over the next 1-3 days, and it will then also be strong enough to lift its head to feed.

I witnessed dozens of hatchings, mostly just glimpses, as on the first occasion, but each one was a privilege. After the new hatchlings dried out from being inside the egg, they quickly gained their slate-grey fluffy coats. The chick's eyes opened during this time, and they learned to lift their heavy heads in order to feed. It can take between one and three days before they are strong enough to receive their first meal. Then with the chick stretching its head high, the adult bird bends over and regurgitates a partly digested soup of krill and fish, rich in oil, the youngsters head disappearing into the maw of its mum or dad. The incredibly gentle parental care of those fragile little creatures was extremely touching and the investment by their parents was clear.

Like the eggs, the tiny chicks were held in the brood pouch. They would not be able to thermoregulate for a few weeks and therefore must be kept warm as well as remaining covered and safe from marauding skuas. This period is known as the guard phase.

The breeding adults now took turns, one brooding and feeding the chicks, the other crossing the fast ice to hunt and return with more food. The weighbridge and tag scanners provided information on how much food was being delivered to the chicks on our marked nests. From that point onwards, food availability and the extent of the fast ice were critical. In bad breeding seasons, which seemed to occur in cycles of four to five years, the fast ice was far more extensive and remained so even into mid-February, late January being the usual break-out time. In addition, food, mainly krill and fish were less available. This had occurred just a few years previously and the result had been catastrophic: 100% chick mortality. My supervisor and I spoke to the researchers that were on Bech at the time and they remained haunted by their experience. Luckily, both for the penguins and therefore for us, this year was looking promising.

Figure 83: The early guard phase. It's a messy and demanding business brooding and guarding two chicks.

When the perfect storm of extensive fast ice (i.e., over 100 kilometres and up to 175 kilometres) and insufficient prey availability strikes, the parent birds have little choice but to abandon their offspring; they must live to breed another year rather than starve to death themselves. Nature can be horribly cruel and walking through the rookery one is conscious of stepping on the bones of the chicks that never made it, a layer several inches deep that represents many breeding seasons. It is both sobering and telling: the pressures that Adélic penguins face in order to procreate are tremendous.

With the parents' guard phase tag-team regimen, the chicks were fed regularly and grew fast. In six weeks, they would increase in weight from about 90 grams to between 2.8 and 3.3 kilograms, an extraordinary energy transfer for a relatively small penguin species that had to travel so far to obtain food.

With regular feeding underway the chicks were revealed more often, and for longer periods, as the adult had to stand up to feed its offspring. I loved watching them feed, one or two chicks now straining upwards for sustenance, tiny flippers stretched out from their bodies, standing on tiptoe. In nests with two chicks, each one received its share, although the first to hatch grew faster. I saw the regurgitated food pass from parent to chick and then swallowed, a look of utter contentment on the chick's visage. The adult gulped back any food that had not been dispensed before once again lying down to cover its offspring.

This was a dangerous time for skua attack as the chicks were exposed during feeding, and they were light enough to be grabbed, almost on the wing and taken away to be swallowed whole. Once again, the wily predators used long learnt tactics to distract and harass the brooding adult while its mate swooped in and grabbed the chick. But it was rarely easily achieved, Adélie penguins with chicks being fierce adversaries. They charged at the avian predators, braying loudly with beak at the ready to tear at the aggressors should they come within striking distance, and perhaps even drag them from the air.

But single penguins, as ferocious as they can be, are often no match for the ingenious teamwork of skuas. Yet at times the penguin won and from then on appeared to be more alert to the presence of skuas when feeding the chicks.

It was always a harrowing sight, seeing chicks being taken and eaten, it happened so fast that I was left reeling, my investment in the penguins biting hard. But skuas have hungry chicks too and as a species they have been part of the ecosystem for thousands of years. I had to remember, that as hard as it was to witness these predation events, skuas generally only account for about 4% of losses. There is also an upside to the loss of one chick out of the two that are usually produced. Single chicks get twice the amount of food and grow much faster and to a greater weight. Their chances of survival to fledging are also increased.

Now, on Bech, it was down to the extent of the fast ice, food availability, and hunting prowess; more experienced Adélies being

Figure 84: Attentive Adélie parents bonding with their chicks.

able to gather sufficient food to sustain both themselves and a chick or chicks. If the fast ice was behaving itself and following the seasonal script by declining a little in extent, there remained the thorny issue of food availability.

There are two species of krill preyed upon by Adélie penguins: crystal krill, that are 2.3 to 3.5 centimetres long, and the larger Antarctic krill that grow to six centimetres in length. Crystal krill live and breed mostly within the continental shelf area, which is also where another favoured prey item, Antarctic silverfish occur. Continental shelves are the flooded margins of continental land masses and are usually less than 100 metres in depth. The Antarctic continental shelf is far deeper at roughly 450 metres deep, dropping down a steep slope to a depth of 1,000 metres. The width of the shelf differs around Antarctica; at Mawson it is between 100 and 120 kilometres wide. Antarctic krill, which are the Adélies preferred prey, are generally found in the deeper water at or beyond the continental shelf.

Antarctic krill are circumpolar in distribution and are the keystone species in the region's food chain; preyed upon by the majority of marine mammals and seabirds that inhabit the area and or breed there during spring and summer. Krill often occur in huge aggregations known as swarms with the total population biomass estimated at 380 million tonnes. However, estimates can be unreliable and annual krill populations vary greatly while the reasons for such variations remain largely unknown.

Marine mammals (especially whales), seabirds, fish and squid take somewhere in the region of 200-million tonnes of Antarctic krill annually. The Convention for the Conservation of Antarctic Resources (CCAMLR) estimates that there is therefore an excess krill biomass of roughly 60-million tonnes.

Figure 85: Antarctic krill Euphausia superba. Critical to the Antarctic food web. Credit: Uwe Kils on Wikimedia Commons.

The human based krill fishery has declined markedly in recent years from a high of 528,000-tonnes to only 100,000-tonnes, mainly because krill are difficult to catch without crushing them in the nets, making them a less saleable product. Methods to overcome this are being researched and should they be successful, scientists will need to advise CCAMLR, the governing body, on sustainable fishing levels. Current Antarctic krill fishery quotas are set at 500,000-tonnes but with a burgeoning world population, demand for protein is likely to create pressure in many areas including on the Antarctic krill fishery.

In relation to krill numbers, there is a strong correlation between the amount and concentration of pack ice and the number and distribution of Antarctic krill. This is because marine algae or phytoplankton, the food of krill, develop and grow on the underside of the pack ice in spring and krill feed on them, using the fissured undersides of the ice as refuges against predation. But if the pack ice is too concentrated or if there is not enough, the density of algae available and therefore the growth and availability of krill to foraging wildlife may be insufficient. Of course, as the season progresses and the ocean warms a little, phytoplankton bloom in the water column and these, often enormous accumulations are fed on by krill swarms. How it all works, especially regarding the pack ice, remains a mystery and scientists are working on the issue because if climate change eventually means less pack ice, it may mean less algae and therefore less krill, causing collapses in a food chain that includes Adélie penguins.

Meanwhile on Bech the evidence that this was a good year for the penguins was recorded by the weighbridge every day; adults were coming and going every three or four days with between 300 and 600 grams of food, the chicks gaining an estimated 80 grams each day.

Figure 86: An Adélie penguin parent feeding its chick. The other chick had already been fed and was snoozing. Note the comb like structures on the adult's tongue and upper palate used for capturing fish and krill.

The guard phase lasts about 22 days and is split between early and late phases. The early phase is when the chicks are brooded, and the latter period is when the youngsters are too large to brood but must still be guarded from predators. There is also intra-specific aggression to consider, and I mentioned previously the fighting and bickering that goes on between Adélies over territory (i.e., the nest site). If a chick wanders into another pair's territory, usually in the late guard phase, it can be pecked to death by the neighbouring breeding adults. It seems merciless I know but it's all about protecting your patch and only feeding your own chicks. Hence the need for parental vigilance.

The hubbub in the rookery, braying adults and whistling chicks, rarely subsided, pausing only as a result of inclement weather, mainly due to the overnight katabatic wind. If represented by a line chart, the sound levels throughout the breeding season would peak when the males were displaying (the ecstatic display) and during pair bonding and mating. But throughout incubation the noise of fights and bickering, together with the strident calls of the skuas could be deafening. Squabbles between adult Adélies also continued throughout the guard phase. It was all part of the breeding cycle and for us the noise was a sign of a healthy rookery.

We had captured some breeding birds from our study nests during the early guard phase in order to attach TDR and satellite tracking devices. To reduce disturbance in the colony and provide us with more space, this procedure was always done away from the rookery, when the adults were either arriving from sea or returning. My supervisor demonstrated the capture technique using the 'net': a canvas bag on a pole. Adélie penguins are smart, they seem to sense one's dastardly purpose and are amazingly fast on their feet. You can find yourself starring in your own comedy sketch, chasing a bird around the shoreline below the colony, as though one is out catching butterflies and not penguins. The skill is in being decisive and fast, to act before the bird suspects, never looking directly at it, and approaching it obliquely rather than directly, then 'whoosh' and the bag is over them. There was usually a scrabble, an attempt to escape, but the catcher would then drop to the ground and hold the bird gently but firmly in the bag between their thighs. If the catcher was my boss, she then passed the bagged bird to me. I was sometimes the catcher but always the holder, my boss being the one who attached the devices. As long as the birds head was covered it did not struggle and seemed to give itself up to our ministrations. We were familiar to the birds, living with them as we did, and I always murmured to them and told them what we were doing and why, which seemed to calm them.

Figure 87: Devices were placed in a direct line with the bird's spine on its lower back, just above the heels in this image. This Adélie was not a target of our ministrations, but I imagined the bird saying to me: 'oy I'm resting here!'

The device, a TDR or a much more expensive satellite tracker was attached low down on the bird's back in order to reduce any underwater 'drag'. My supervisor rubbed quick-setting glutinous grey glue into the stiff feathers and placed the device, pressing it firmly to ensure good adhesion. Once the glue set, I held the bird upright, head still covered by the bag and a number, often with a letter first, was spray painted on its breast. For some reason I remember T13: a lucky number? Then we sat quietly for a short spell to allow the bird to get over the indignity of the procedure, before releasing it towards the fast ice. The bird quickly hopped away on the rock but then stopped, did a full body shake and then went about its business seemingly no worse for wear. Penguins don't hold grudges; they live in the moment and carry on where they left off.

The penguins carrying devices were, apart from the longer trips during incubation, only at sea for three or four days although they might do more than one trip before the TDR or satellite tracker was retrieved. The trick was in catching them before they returned to their nest as doing so in the colony would be highly disruptive. Surveillance was constant and we usually saw them coming as they reached the shore; otherwise, we had to wait once again until they

Figure 88: Penguins, including the Adélie are beautifully adapted to their underwater life while also allowing them to walk upright. Seeing them 'fly' so fast underwater was a revelation to me.

were leaving. Following capture, the device was carefully removed using a scalpel to avoid any unnecessary damage to its feathers. Any residual glue would be cast-off during the seasonal moult when the birds gained a new suit of feathers.

It takes several years of deploying a few TDRs and satellite trackers annually to gain a true picture of where the different sexes are going during the various phases of breeding and plotting their dive profiles at the feeding grounds. But what was becoming apparent is that while Adélie penguins can dive to a staggering 180 metres, most dives are within 50 metres of the surface, the majority of those being to 20 metres or less. This may be because Adélies hunt mainly in the evening when krill migrate towards the surface, the crustaceans having been at 100 metres depth throughout the day to avoid predation. Dive duration is usually two to five minutes and Adélie penguins generally dive in bouts of 10-20 dives. They repeat these dive bouts 30-40 times on each trip with brief rests in between. Adélies may therefore dive between 300 and 800 times on a single trip, depending on prey availability.

Penguins are beautifully streamlined for their largely underwater lifestyle and can 'fly' at eight kilometres per hour. Unlike flying seabirds, penguins are subject to great underwater pressure, so their bones are solid. They can restrict blood flow to peripheral areas and to non-essential organs and they produce large amounts of haemoglobin, (the oxygen carrying element in red blood cells), allowing them to dive deeper and for longer. They mostly catch their prey by sight but can also sense them using fine hairs near their bill. The backward facing barbs on the Adélie's tongue and upper mandible both grasp the prey and strain out the seawater. With such speed underwater and their specific adaptations, I would not want to be a fish with an Adélie penguin on my tail!

When the females go to sea after laying their eggs, they remain away for roughly two weeks and satellite trackers have shown that they travel well beyond the continental shelf. Having expended a huge amount of energy producing eggs, they must replace the body fat that was consumed. To do this their preferred prey is Antarctic krill which swarm in deep water. In contrast, while the males have fasted for two weeks or so they have not lost as much weight. They therefore forage in shallower waters much more locally, preying mainly on crystal krill and Antarctic silverfish.

Once the chicks hatch, both sexes hunt at or near the continental shelf margin, feeding on a mixture of Antarctic krill and fish, the females usually taking more krill than the males. The chicks are fed by the adult guarding them with frequent changeovers when the other parent returns from foraging.

My boss and I travelled to and from station several times during the various breeding phases, although during the busy guard phase we stayed on base for only two to three days at a time. Washing clothes on Bech was awkward and the station was only four kilometres away, with hot showers always extremely alluring. At times, the period on station might allow for field trips. If we had to get back to the island to carry out a count or particularly timely observations, it was easy enough to accomplish.

We always returned with some fresh meat and whatever vegetables (mostly frozen) that were available on station. Steak or chicken and vegetables was a welcome change from tinned produce, of which we had an almost endless supply. Even butter came in tins.

My favourite meal on Bech was a Fray Bentos tinned steak and kidney pie, tinned new potatoes and peas. We had plenty of dried food too, pasta and rice, flour, milk powder and cereals. I learnt to bake bread, the living pod full of the mouth-watering smell, great anticipation until we cut steaming slices and had them with butter and jam. There were scones and pancakes, even crumbles and rice puddings, we certainly never went hungry.

It was now just before Christmas and the first batch of TDRs and satellite tracking devices had been recovered. We would deploy a second batch of devices during the late guard phase but for now our job was done. Before leaving Bech we counted the chicks, 1,829 chicks had survived from an original 1,933 nests with eggs: a fantastic result. Buoyed by the news we prepared to leave Bech to take part in the festivities on station. There would be time to phone home and send some emails as well as developing more photos. Changing out of our outer layer of work clothes, now rather smelly from penguin poo (we kept them in the storehouse), we collected our laundry and burnable rubbish and headed off over the ice to station.

Figure 89: Returning to station after two weeks on Bech, a hot shower in our sights. My supervisor walking while I skied.

CHAPTER 12:

FESTIVE SEASON

The most celebrated day of the year on Australian Antarctic stations is mid-winters day, because from then on, the days very gradually lengthen which in turn leads to the return of the sun. This festive tradition has been in place since the first British explorers over-wintered on the continent and the same pantomime, Cinderella is enacted, some men dressing as women to great acclaim and uproarious laughter.

Figure 90: The bar and lounge area festooned with tinsel. The Christmas tree is over by the window. Credit: Andy Burgess.

Christmas comes a close second and any groups working remotely at field camps return to base so that everyone is present for the special event. Many expeditioners hailed from parts of Australia where snow was unheard of but this year, we were all guaranteed a white Christmas.

Everyone pulled together to make it a special day; a day to remember. A traditionally decorated Christmas tree graced the upstairs lounge while tinsel and streamers festooned the ceiling, and carols played on the sound system.

There was a barbeque on Christmas eve in the newly constructed workshop, another large red shed, but a baby compared to the accommodation block. There was homebrew beer and hot glühwein and standing around a space heater we sang carols to the best of our ability.

Santa's arrival at the red shed on a quad bike and trailer commenced the Christmas day celebrations. Looking suitably snowy-bearded and chubby, and adorned in the traditional ermine trimmed red suit, he was lustily cheered, and the banter flowed freely. Painted and tinselled wooden reindeer antlers decorated the quad bikes handlebars with the trailer similarly decorated, the latter loaded with sacks of presents. After many photos were snapped both the sacks and Santa were carried shoulder high to the door of the red shed.

Every year there is a station Christmas present lottery, each person pulling out a name from a hat and either making a gift in one of the stations workshops or giving a gift brought from home for that purpose. Nothing expensive, a gesture gift only, although some made on base were quite elaborate.

The presents were emptied from the sacks and installed below the glittering tree and once Santa had been fortified by a stiff whisky, he took his seat by the tree. As each name was called the recipient was expected to sit on Santa's lap to receive their gift. There was great laughter and ribaldry as the presents were given out and many more photos and videos taken.

A champagne brunch started the feasting, only a precursor to a later dinner but with platters of bacon, eggs, sausages and black pudding as well as freshly made croissants, bagels, seafood and cold meats and even some salad from the station hydroponics hut. Champagne corks were popped, bouncing off the ceiling and everyone was well oiled by the meal's conclusion. Once the table was cleared and the washing up complete most folk wandered off to phone their loved ones and to rest up for the evening's festivities.

From mid-afternoon onwards many people either helped the chef in the kitchen or prepared the table in the upstairs lounge for dinner. Red tablecloths, fake holly and ivy, tinsel, and candles adorned the table, wine glasses and cutlery reflected the Christmas lights and candles.

Everyone was dressed in their best and we gathered around the bar for pre-dinner drinks. An elaborate meal followed: turkey, chicken, glazed hams, roasted vegetables, stuffing, the works. We all wore silly party hats and the pistol shots of crackers exploded around the large table. We ate and drank too much and while some of the jollity was a little forced that was only to be expected; it was all in the nature of being far from home. There is great camaraderie and collaboration on Antarctic bases and Mawson was no exception, everyone helped in the clean-up following Christmas dinner and then mostly retired having eaten and drunk too much.

One day during the Christmas period I persuaded one of the electricians to travel with me over the ice to Welch Island about five kilometres northeast of station. Travelling alone is not permitted so I had to find a willing participant and during the festive season the bar is a magnet and prising folk away from it can be difficult. I felt very gratified when my companion agreed to go as Welch Island has a summit of 130-metres, the highest in Holme Bay. It also has the largest Adélie penguin rookery in the region with about 20,000 breeding pairs.

It was an after-dinner evening excursion, so we only had about three hours before the katabatic wind potentially kicked in. Quad bike travel on fast ice is easy and we crossed the five kilometres in about 15-minutes. Leaving Horseshoe Harbour, we passed the Jocelyn Island group and approached the Klung Islands of which Welch Island is the largest. We rode to Welch Island's north-western side which slopes gently down to the shoreline, making access from the fast ice easier (please see next page for map and end of chapter for an image).

It was a perfect evening, the sun on its downward journey in a cirrus wreathed sky, zero wind and only about minus four-degrees.

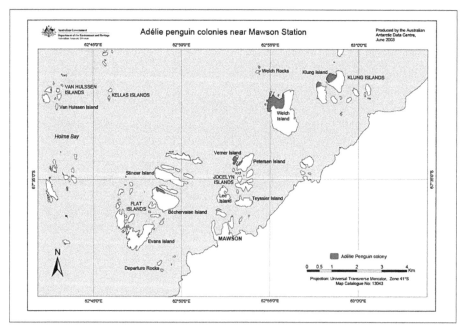

Figure 90: Welch Island (north-east of Mawson) is the largest of the Holme Bay islands and has the biggest Adélie penguin rookery (shown in dark grey). Credit: Australian Antarctic Division.

This was the time of almost perpetual sunset and sunrise before the great golden orb climbed back into the sky, never having broken the horizon.

Close to shore there were huge ice pressure ridges and as it was now late December the tide cracks had opened and were full of sea water. Scores of Adélie penguins were bathing, thrashing and splashing in one great exuberant mass of birds; the business of guarding and feeding chicks made far more pleasant with meltwater nearby. Penguins eat ice to hydrate, and with soft slushy snow available due to above zero temperatures during the day, their appreciation was evident.

Leaving the quads on firm ice we found a place to jump from the ice onto the island, a leap of about a metre which my long-legged companion jumped with ease. We followed the shore, skirting the penguin colonies, their raucous calls following us, and approached the summit ridge from the southwest. Welch Island, like many other areas around Mawson is a geologist's dream with some of the oldest rocks on the planet that have various erratics, extrusions and dykes to explore. All of the Holme Bay islands are rugged: great slabs and mounds of granite that have been split by ice and littered with huge rocks and boulders left behind by the ice sheet when it retreated thousands of years ago.

We climbed slowly up the long ridge on sure-footed granite, a strenuous but enjoyable ascent. Having stopped to enjoy the penguins in their joyful bathing we reached the summit an hour after leaving station. And what a summit it is! The 360-degree panorama is another of Mawson's great treasures. Many say (and I wholeheartedly agree) that Mawson is the jewel in the Australian Antarctic Territory crown, the variety of experiences on offer unparalleled by Casey or Davis.

Figure 92: Snow melt provided slushy snow for thirsty Adélie penguins. Note the tidal pressure ridges in the background ice.

We sat up there as though on a great throne, the cloud providing a vast canvas for the setting sun, a pallet of colours seen nowhere else. From pale straw to golden egg-yolk yellow, salmon pink through to crimson and vermillion, sapphire blue to azure, lilacs and mauves deepening to violets, pink blushed icebergs and fast ice stretching to the horizon. Behind us lay burnished blue ice cliffs, the Mount Henderson massif gilded and glowing on the alabaster plateau.

All around us flew two dozen or more snow petrels, swooping and turning, dark eyes watching us closely, sometimes alighting briefly in small groups on nearby rock-slabs. We were far enough away from their nests not to alarm them but close enough that they were compelled through curiosity to check us out. The clamour of tens of thousands of Adélie penguins drifted up the slopes from below. We could see the rookery marked out in pale coloured guano and though we could not smell it from our perch, I had plenty of experience to imagine the delightful bouquet.

Our surroundings and the presence of the snow petrels was quite literally mind blowing and my companion said that he was glad that I had suggested the trip. We sat up there for an hour with the sunset going on and on, changing only subtly, the colours melding and blending in a tapestry of light. Like many of my experiences in Antarctica it could not last long enough, the need to return to station before the katabatic wind kicked-in being imperative. But then what is enough? Just to be there was beyond my wildest dreams, I could never have imagined it, being on that airy throne not far off midnight with the ivory birds all around us in a land made of ice amidst the world's greatest wilderness, largely untouched by humanity.

Figure 93: One of 30 or 40 snow petrels that flew around us like giant confetti as we sat on Welch Island's summit.

We returned to station, somehow better people, more space in our beings, and more at peace.

On New Year's Eve there was a smorgasbord of take-away food. There were burgers and French fries, pizzas, fried chicken and curries with rice and pappadums. It may seem strange but most of us craved fast-food, so easily accessed in that world far to the north. It somehow bestowed some normality to this land far away.

Close to midnight and we were all either around the bar or in the adjacent lounge. I was feeling mighty fine after three gin and tonics with glacier ice and several shots of black sambuca. The countdown to midnight started and we all joined in, shouting the numbers to the rooftop. We wished one another a happy new year and two mostly sober blokes set off some fireworks outside; we could just hear the percussions and see the flashes from the window. Then came a rather drunken rendition of Auld Lang Syne. It was a new year in Antarctica.

We left for Bech on January 2ⁿᵈ knowing that this could be the last time that we walked and or skied over the fast ice. Regular checks on ice thickness were conducted on Horseshoe Harbour and the

Figure 94: The volcano-like cone of Welch Island after the break-up of the fast ice. Some of the Jocelyn Islands are in the centre of the frame with the icesheet in the foreground.

latest measurement showed that it was now only 0.7-metre thick and thinning quite rapidly. We thought that we might just get another return journey to station in before the station leader deemed the ice unsafe. Once that happened, we would be on Bech until the ice broke-out which usually occurred in late January or early February.

CHAPTER 13:

ICE AND SNOW ESCAPADES

A GRAND DAY OUT

On Boxing Day eight people piled into two Hägglunds vehicles, four to each, while four others climbed onto quad bikes, and we roared off up to the plateau. This was to be our grand day out, a rare event at Mawson, given that most field parties were comprised of only four people due to field hut capacity. This was different; we were out for the day only, returning to station in the evening. Each Hägglunds towed a trailer packed with coloured plastic sledges, both cross country and downhill skis together with associated paraphernalia including some tow ropes and finally our lunch.

The tracked vehicles chugged up the slope while the quads raced ahead sometimes returning to the slower vehicles before tearing off again. It was a beautiful calm sunny summers day, close to zero degrees, and as it was the day after Christmas a few expeditioners, those in the Häggs, were nursing hangovers. Some of the freshest air on the planet was called for as well as vigorous exercise.

We pulled up at a long snow-covered slope near Fischer Nunatak, about three kilometres south of Mount Henderson. The glare was intense, and sunglasses were a must, the snow reflecting 90% of the light. The nunatak reared up like a great brown pyramid, the nut-

Figure 95: Skiers and tobogganers waiting for a ride as the Hägglunds returns from dropping off another group, some of whom can just be seen on the hilltop while two others ski downhill to the right of the hill.

brown rock surrounded by blue ice, the nearby snow slope perfect for skiing and tobogganing. Hendo lay behind us with the Masson range to our right and the David Range beyond.

There were half a dozen one-person plastic sledges, enough cross-country skis and boots for four and two pairs of downhill skis with a small selection of boots.

So, time for the fun to begin! A dozen people, some flying down the slope on sledges, others skiing nearby, two quads acting as tows, taking the skiers back to the top. It was only a 30-second ride on downhill skis but where better to do it: the Antarctic plateau! I found it so much easier to ski downhill, carving turns on the downward slope although I took a turn on cross-country skis and practised my telemark turns, slowly getting better at them.

Figure 96: The fun of tobogganing. The furthest black speck is a skier, while the others are tobogganers. The tracks of the Hägglunds are clearly visible.

There was the 'swoosh' of skis and toboggans, mixed with yells, shouts and laughter as folk collided on the sledges or fell over on skis, hangovers forgotten in the great Antarctic outdoors. I joined five others as we tobogganed down the slope in a line, trying to remain abreast, arms across those beside us. It didn't work of course, ending in a heap of laughing, snow covered bodies at the bottom. Spontaneous snowball fights broke out and everyone joined in, using the Häggs as shelter from a pelting.

The bright yellow Häggs, crimson-coloured quad bikes, plastic sledges in various shades and our red, yellow, green and royal blue clothing contrasted with the predominant pale blue and white hues all around us. The sun shone down out of an azure sky, witness to twelve people having fun, whooping and laughing, totally free, thousands of kilometres from the complicated busy world to our north.

We had brought lunch from station, leftovers from Christmas: chicken legs, honey-glazed ham and gouda cheese on fresh-made rolls; and moist Christmas cake with flasks of hot coffee and glühwein to follow. We sat in rows leaning up against the Hägglunds gazing out at the view, chatting excitedly about our best sledging and ski runs and describing falls and face plants in the snow.

Some rested after lunch, while the others tobogganed and skied until they too were tired. The temperature had risen during the day and was now two degrees above freezing. Most folk had cast off a layer or two of clothing and had faces adorned in white zinc cream as though on an Aussie beach. The snow had become less suitable for sledging as it melted, so in mid-afternoon we packed up and headed back towards station.

The lead Hägg took us to the left away from the drum line and across to a flattish area of blue ice. We discovered a sizeable melt stream,

Figure 97: The cleanest, freshest and oldest water on the planet! Melt streams and lakes are common on the plateau during summer. They are beautiful to look at and sit beside. Two of the traverse trailers at GWAMM can just be seen top-right and the tip of Hendo to the left of them.

half a metre wide and deep, the water running fast towards the coast, carving its way through the ice. Melt streams and lakes are common during summer when positive temperatures occur. They cascade off the ice cliffs down onto patches of open water far below, the sound of gushing waterfalls a new experience for us all.

We filled our water bottles with the world's freshest, cleanest water, ready chilled and from at least 100,000-year-old glacial ice that had flowed there from the inland icecap. Standing around in little more than thermal underwear we enjoyed the warmth while looking all around at the gleaming water slicked icesheet. Far below the fast ice was melting too, the surface cratered by melt pools.

That night on station we had gin and tonics with blue ice chipped by ice axe from the plateau. As it melted it cracked with tiny pistol shots, captive air bubbles trapped inside for millennia escaping with a fanfare. We toasted our grand day out and Antarctica. It was a fine end to a marvellously memorable day.

ICE YACHT ADVENTURE

A carpenter who had been at Mawson when the huskies were there and who had regaled me with stories of dog sledding on the fast ice asked if I would like to try ice yachting sometime. To make up for the loss of the huskies he had designed and helped build a steel ice-yacht which was sailed on Horseshoe Harbour. The yacht was built of angle and boxed steel left over from building projects and welded together by a competent welder with a plywood platform for sitting on and a steel mast that supported a specially adapted brightly coloured sail. It was a real beast, weighing over a tonne, but highly effective on the ice.

A week or so later, in mid-November, whilst the harbour ice was still over 1.5 metres thick, I saw the yacht flying over the ice, two people on board. I wandered down to the harbour and out onto the ice to watch them, It was a fine day though cloudy, about minus 15 degrees with a 20-knot easterly, plenty of wind for the event. The yacht was powering away from me, heading for the far shore of the harbour and I wondered whether it had a brake or some way of stopping. My question was answered when on approaching the far shore the sail was loosened, flapping in the wind, and the yacht turned a wide semi-circle with the remaining momentum and now faced back the way it had come. It was expertly done, as was the way in which the sail was quickly re-tensioned, and the vessel thundered back towards me without stopping. It looked incredible and somewhat frightening, and while I wanted to leave in case they beckoned me onboard, I was rooted to the spot.

As the yacht neared me, I could see two grinning blokes onboard having a great time as it sped over the ice. They released the lanyard and turned the yacht around then stopped and called me over. Oh god I thought, here we go!

Ensconced on the plywood deck my two friends showed me where to sit and how the sail worked, the rope running through two cleats, secured in the steel frame. There was no brake, so control of the yacht was purely by harnessing the air, using a rudder like device to turn the skis and then, once near the other end releasing the air from the sail and using the momentum to turn the heavy beast around. Brilliantly simple and terrifyingly rudimentary.

Off we went, literally thundering over the ice, which appeared to be smooth but was not, the juddering motion blurring our vision, shaking us to the core as we reached terminal velocity. I was both almost shitting my pants whilst simultaneously feeling exhilarated, especially as the far shore loomed rapidly before me, the rock and ice blurring together so that I couldn't with any accuracy see where one ended and the other began. What some people do for fun! It was mad and yet tremendously exciting.

We made a couple more runs and then suddenly I was being offered the reins. Apparently the four runs they had made with me on board was my training, but they had never said as much to me. I protested, telling them that I didn't even know how to sail but with no success, they moved over and handed me the lanyard, telling me it was easy. 'Just pull on the rope they said, and at the other end release it, while one of us works the rudder'. What could possibly go wrong? I tried once more to protest but failed to impress upon them my lack of courage in the face of overwhelming terror.

Pulling on the rope they yelled 'that's enough!' and we were off, rapidly gaining momentum, the juddering once again blurring my vision as we screamed over the ice, or was that me screaming, I think it was! It was vastly different being the one in control, or nominally so. The rate of travel was mind blowing, the far shore looming so quickly. I was frozen in position, frozen in terror, while they screamed 'let go, LET GO!'

Their desperate shouting penetrated my fear, but I let go too slowly and there was a loud tearing sound as the sail tore down the middle and the yacht slewed around, one runner coming off the ice and then thumping back down, as it came to a sudden halt.

I think we were all stunned, I certainly was. I was gabbling unintelligibly, apologising, having destroyed their sail. After a brief hiatus when they looked somewhat horrified, they started laughing and said not to worry, they had a spare sail.

We had to manually haul the yacht back to the shore below station where it was winched onto a trailer that looked as though it had been purpose built of similar steel. Ice yachting was another experience like none that had gone before, another first for me, and something I would remember forever. Antarctica was full of firsts. I found out later that there was no spare sail and that it took hours of hand stitching to fix the tear.

Sadly, I did not have my camera with me for this event, so cannot share any photos.

BEETLE MANIA

One day in late-November I was upstairs in the red shed's lounge looking out of the north facing window when I saw a surprising sight: a strange looking vehicle that I had never seen before doing donuts on the harbour ice.

I kitted up and walked out into a fine though overcast day, the temperature minus 17 degrees. With Antarctica's super dry air, it never felt as cold to me as the cold damp air of the Scottish or Tasmanian highlands. The very adequate clothing that was provided by the Australian Antarctic Division kept me perfectly warm on most occasions.

Strolling down to the harbour I could see that the vehicle was just a chassis (no body) with rear mounted air-cooled engine and two front seats, the roll bar over the open cabin making it look like an over-sized dune buggy.

The driver, the vehicles sole occupant, in sledging hat and ski goggles gunned the Volkswagen (VW) over the ice and put it into a long 180-degree slide. It did so gracefully, a mass of steel with seemingly unstoppable momentum. The driver kept the vehicle in motion, coming out of one slide only to gun it over the ice and into another. On the return leg I think he saw me watching because he executed a beautiful handbrake slide through 360 degrees. He obviously knew what he was doing, manoeuvring the stripped-down car in a way that was like poetry in motion, an ice dance of sorts. The vehicle pirouetted and spun, roared across the ice and spun again, over and over.

Figure 98: I did not have my camera with me on the day and taking pictures of the buggy wasn't encouraged anyway. Here is the chassis of a VW beetle. Imagine it with two front brown leather seats and a roll bar just behind the seats. And a steering wheel of course! credit: ChengH on Wikimedia Commons.

Fifteen minutes later the car - if you could call it such - pulled up alongside me and the driver jumped out, the engine still running. Removing his hat and goggles and revealing himself as a friend of mine, he asked me if I'd like to have a go. I said yes immediately, forgetting any qualms I should have had about climate change. He showed me the manual controls and then shifting over to the passenger seat beckoned me into the driver's position.

We spent a few minutes as I got used to the pedals and adjusted the seat. Apparently, the brakes were not great - I was assured that I wouldn't need them - but that the engine was tip top.

I had never had an opportunity to do donuts or handbrake turns before but it turned out to be easy on ice: a turn of the wheel for a 180-degree slide and that plus the handbrake for the 360. I was schooled for five minutes and then my mate deemed me ready to fly solo and after explaining where to park up the vehicle once I was done, he climbed out and headed back up to his workshop.

My moves were tentative at first, but I quickly grew in confidence. The harbour is sizeable enough for the 95-metre-long resupply ship and so for a car on the ice there was acres of space and no danger of hitting the rock edges. I was soon flying over the ice and in my borrowed sledging hat and goggles I felt like an early racing car driver, the wind in my face and the goggles creating tunnel vision. The air-cooled VW Beetle rear-mounted engine had plenty of power, the rear-wheel-drive perfect for the ice.

I'm not a petrol head but this was exceptional and exhilarating open air driving, powering over the ice then taking her into slides and turns, travelling between two large blue ice rinks, the speed creating the momentum required. Having the engine behind me rather than in front made a huge difference and being enclosed by roll bars I felt quite safe.

I found out much later that Mawson station had a long history with Volkswagen Beetles. The first vehicle, dubbed 'Antarctica 1' arrived at Mawson in February 1963, to supplement much slower transport. Beetles were being specially manufactured and promoted for Arctic regions and this ruby-red vehicle was loaned to ANARE as a marketing ploy. It worked spectacularly, the car that many had believed incapable of driving up to the plateau did the return journey

Figure 99: Antarctica 1: the 'Red Terror' on the fast ice near Mawson. Credit: Geoff Merrill.

of 35-kilometres to the (then) Rumdoodle ice runway in just over 50 minutes. Christened the 'Red Terror', the vehicle's journey was filmed, and many still shots were also taken against Antarctic back-drops with the film then sent back on the ship to the people at Volkswagen. The footage and images were a sensation in Australia and VW Beetle and Camper Van sales hit record highs. After great service at Mawson station, Antarctica 1 was returned to Australia and competed in a rally which it won. The vehicles all-round credentials were firmly established, and this added to its much-loved reputation worldwide.

Antarctica 2 replaced the red terror at Mawson and Antarctica 3 followed, both vehicles being orange in colour. They provided excellent service, especially via shuttling Russian pilots and crew between the ice runway at Rumdoodle and station. The fame of the Mawson VW

Beetles carried far and wide and when the AAD withdrew them from service and sent them back to Australia, their loss was keenly felt. Fortunately, at that time, if there was room on the ship, expeditioners could have personal vehicles shipped to the Antarctic stations. On two occasions VW Beetles were shipped to Mawson and the station's close association with the vehicle continued.

Then in the 1980s personal vehicles were no longer allowed on station and those already there were to be sent back.

Sadly, one of the Beetles was already lost: it had broken though a thin patch of fast ice and sank to the sea floor in many fathoms of water not far from Mawson; driver and passenger okay. The AAD attempted to repatriate the other vehicle but every time a resupply vessel arrived at Mawson the car mysteriously vanished. Most expeditioners, both past and present, knew where the car was hidden during resupply, but nobody ever spilled the beans.

The remaining Beetle was stripped and rebuilt without its bodywork and now there was I, driving it, cutting donuts and 360-degree handbrake turns on the ice of Horseshoe Harbour. If I had known the history of the Mawson VWs it would certainly have enhanced my experience but driving the car on that day, the freedom and exhilaration it gave me, is another memory of Mawson that will remain with me always.

CHAPTER 14:

RUMDOODLING

Expedition Rumdoodle rolled out of station one Friday afternoon in early December. My companions were the three geologists that I got along so well with and who had become friends. We tore off up the plateau on quad bikes in a line, one behind the other.

Rumdoodle is defined as: 'an event or happening that is ultimately a success despite the complete incompetence of all those involved in its planning and execution.' W.E. Bowman employed this rationale when he published a short book in 1956 parodying non-fictional mountaineering expeditions where the incompetent proponents climbed an imaginary 40,000foot peak named Rum Doodle.

As a result of this parody a mountain in the North Masson Range near Mawson station was named Rumdoodle.

In our group there were two experienced climbers, and two like me that had climbed only a little. Being afraid of exposed heights (I'm fine on scrambles and on mountain tops) I drove myself to climb, partly in order not to seem weak, but also because the views from the top were often exceptional. I knew that I might only be in Antarctica once and I was determined to conquer my fear to climb this wonderfully named peak. What could possibly go wrong?!

Reaching GWAMM we followed the cane line route to the North Masson range. Crossing dimpled blue ice on quads is best done at speed because it evens out the irregular surface and reduces the jarring effect on machine and rider. One must avoid any sideways sliding movement as the rippled ice can cause vehicles to tip over.

We rode up and over the icesheet undulations drawing closer to the North Masson Range. To our right, about 10-kilometres away, lay the David Range with Fang Peak living up to its iconic name. At this time of year, the sun does not set but follows a constant parabolic curve, just grazing the horizon before rising again. As the sun descended that evening it cast longer shadows, each bike and rider having their own phantom presence.

Arriving at Rumdoodle hut, known to all expeditioners past and present as Maxine's, we unpacked and claimed a bunk each. After a hot cuppa we grabbed the climbing gear and practiced roping up, each of us wearing a harness with carabiner attached. The nearby crags provided an easy pitch, nothing too hairy, and in fact it was fun, scrambling up and then abseiling down. But I knew that next day's climb would challenge my equilibrium and just as during field training, I would most likely have to wrestle with fear.

It was a fine night in the hut, good food brought from station and a rare glass or two of red wine in great company. A weekend away from station politics and gossip was just what the doctor ordered. Amongst ourselves the banter was gentle and uncomplicated, conversation flowed from topic to topic mostly regarding mountains we had climbed and wilderness areas we had walked in as well as the wildlife that lived there. They were curious about my life on Bech and working with Adélie penguins while they tried to teach me about Antarctic geology and geologic time in relation to what we saw all around us. Understanding that East Antarctica is an area of continental shield and that most of the rock is over three billion years old was astounding although I struggled to comprehend a timespan of even a thousand years.

Figure 100: Maxines. Note the heavy-duty steel retaining cables. The hut was completely blown away on one occasion and has been badly damaged on other occasions due to hurricane force winds on the plateau that are amplified by the hut's proximity to almost vertical cliffs.

It was a perfect blue-sky day for the climb, not a cloud to be seen, minus ten degrees and no wind. We were all tooled up in harnesses, our most experienced member with a jangling belt of carabiners, belay and rappelling devices. Each of us wore a coloured helmet. There was no shortage of climbing equipment at Mawson, and we had checked out all that was needed for our epic adventure.

Dry granite makes for an excellent climbing surface, hand and footholds were easy to find. If we adhered to the golden rule: three points of contact, everything flowed smoothly, and we were soon up the crags and onto Rumdoodle proper.

Now with great tilted slabs of rock to climb it got a little hairier and I felt a bit of a wobble in the knees. Experienced climbers always tell those who are afraid not to look down. The advice flies in the face of normal human impulse. On previous climbs no matter how hard I tried not to, I always ending up looking down. Of course, as soon as I looked down between my legs, I felt my guts clench and the sweat chill as it broke out on my back and forehead. But I kept going, born onwards and upwards by male pride, something that has at times saved men's lives but much more frequently killed them. I soon discovered that the other novice climber was as terrified as I was, and that solidarity helped me to overcome some of my fear. Luckily the two experienced climbers were the sort that understood fear of heights and so talked us through the holds whenever we needed moral support.

A couple of long pitches and we reached a ledge wide enough for the four of us to congregate and look at the incredible views over the icecap, along the North Masson Range and across blue ice to the David Range. I realised that the vista from the summit must be extraordinary, and the thought provided the impetus for me to keep going, as this might be my only opportunity to achieve what for me was my Everest. So far, the Rumdoodle definition had not come to pass, our two experienced climbers being very competent leaders.

Next came a long upward sloping ledge that cut a massive slab in two, the uphill part providing handholds, the lower part a sharp drop onto boulders. The ledge was just wide enough to walk along carefully which we did roped up and belayed. The ledge provided exceptional views of Rumdoodle's very striking secondary peak: South Doodle. A brief scramble then took us to the summit slabs. The ranges that comprise the Framne mountains emerge through the icecap so that the remaining elevations to be climbed are only 300-500 metres although like Rumdoodle, it was not always easy. Regardless, it does not really matter when you are on a 60-metre-high rock slab tilted at

45 to 50-degrees, looking down between your legs at unfriendly looking boulders.

We made it though. Two more pitches and a scramble and I emerged on top to be joined by the others being belayed. Success without incompetence: not a true Rumdoodle but I and my exposed heights-challenged friend felt as though we had climbed that imaginary 40,000½ foot peak. Conquering fear and ending up on top of the world when at the bottom of the world was magnificent and the views as ever were extraordinary. Snow petrels flew around our heads and the sun was high in an azure sky.

Figure 101: After a brief rest climbers traverse the ledge that splits the massive slab in two on Mount Rumdoodle. Beyond is the spire of South Doodle.

The scale of the place was mind boggling. An ice sheet of epic proportions with Hendo to our northeast, the David Range to the west and the Casey Range far beyond. The Central and South Masson's lay to the south and away in the distance was Mount Hordern and the Brown Range. All around there was blue ice or brighter snow-covered ice tongues and wind scours. Several of the peaks had been climbed in 1956 by a party led by John Béchervaise for whom Béchervaise Island was named.

From our vantage point the transition between icecap and fast ice (of which we could see only a sliver) was all but invisible, just ice as far as we could see topped by pale blue sky.

Figure 102: Looking southwest from Mount Rumdoodle's summit with Mount Hordern prominent at top right. Part of the Brown Range can only just be seen at top left.

We remained on the summit for 45-minutes, although I could have stayed hours. I was also trying to ignore the inescapable fact that what goes up must come down. Using figure of eight devices, we roped up and abseiled down the first pitches. Even though scared on ascents of sheer exposed rock, I much prefer climbing up to abseiling down because one does not have to lean out backwards over the abyss and trust that the rope won't snap. Now my legs really did start to shake. "Lean back, lean back it's easier" were the encouraging calls. And it *was* easier but try telling my brain that. The adrenalin kicked in with only two available choices: continue on down or stay where I was and freeze-up (and probably cry). I chose 'down' and after the initial lean outwards and the beginning of my descent I was able to relax a little and even enjoy it a little, well the last pitch at least.

Being back on solid ground was delightful. I had done it, I had climbed Rumdoodle! We high-fived, especially the two of us who had been petrified, and then divested of climbing tackle, we enjoyed a very welcome hot cuppa and cheese, salami and biscuits on the deck of the hut. After being so tense on the descent my muscles slowly relaxed and we relived the climb's critical moments, the two of us who had been shit-scared now able to laugh at our fear.

Rejuvenated, we decided to take a ride over to Fang Peak Hut in the David Range. It was only 10-kilometres distant and on quads we were there in half an hour. We had all been there during field training, but it was great to see it again. The sky had become almost overcast and the ice was a magical patchwork of light and shade.

Beyond the hut to the west lay a wide bowl of ice and a huge field of hexagonal shapes etched in rock and ice. Each one was about 20-30-metres across and there were about 40 or 50 of them. The geologists were fascinated, they had heard of these post glacial structures and many photos were snapped of them.

Figure 103: Looking down from the slopes of Fang Peak to the hut of the same name. Another group were camping there, hence the polar pyramid tents. Note the hexagonal shapes referred to in the text above.

Leaving the quads, we scrambled up onto the ridge, part way up Fang Peak which requires ropes to reach the final summit. It provided another perspective on the plateau and mountains, with a view eastward to the Masson ranges as well as a great view south to Mount Hordern, and beyond to the great white desert. Every view is different, that is why I climb mountains, the exercise being a bonus. When alone I always spend at least an hour on mountain summits; why expend all that energy only to turn around after a few minutes and descend! There's generally so much to see. We were less than a third the way up Fang Peak, but the views were nevertheless exceptional.

As we descended a breeze sprang up, but we thought nothing of it as it was far too early for the katabatic wind, and blizzards were rare in summer, although we were only into the early days of December. If we had been more aware we would have noted the easterly direction, a cyclonic stream rather than a more southerly katabatic.

We set off back to Maxine's and were halfway there when conditions deteriorated. We realised too late that we might be in for a drubbing. Our climbing gear, books and toiletries were all still at Maxine's and as we were already at the halfway mark we pressed on. The wind was rising fast, and spindrift danced and swirled across the ice and around our machines. Suddenly we were enveloped, visibility reduced to zero in patches, then easing a little so that we could see further. The air was thick with flying snow and ice particles.

Knowing that we were in trouble we quickly donned our ski goggles, leaving the tinted visors up for better visibility. Our lead climber on Rumdoodle was quickly designated leader and he shouted over the howling wind to remember our field training and not to panic. He told us to wait until we saw his lights before proceeding and to stick together. He reminded us that if a machine stopped and could not be started, we should leave it and double up; survival was all.

We had stopped at a drum marker and while three of us remained, the leader drove forwards, disappearing into the howling maelstrom. Visibility in blizzards often varies and so it was with this one, changing from white out to a few metres and now and then out to 50 and even 100-metres. In this way the lead bike edged forwards, stopping when visibility dropped and proceeding when it improved. After several minutes we saw his headlight as he turned his quad bike through 180-degrees pointing back in our direction having reached the next drum marker. We proceeded as he had, slowly, and in a line abreast, so that nobody could be missed in white-out and or left behind with a stalled vehicle.

It was a frightening experience and I think we all felt moments of panic, although most of those realisations came later. In the moment we were all sharply focussed on moving safely forward. It had been drilled into us during training that in blizzards panic can kill, the decisions made often being erroneous and leading to potentially fatal actions. On station, where there are 'blizz lines' there had been cases of expeditioners getting momentarily lost within a few metres of safety.

Out there in the blizzard we were minuscule bundles of flesh, blood and bone, protected only by many layers of insulated clothing and totally dependent on our machines not failing us. If more than one quad bike ceased to function, the air intake blocked by snow and ice, we would have been in dire straits. Luckily for us our steeds continued onwards, with only the odd cough from an engine as they struggled to breathe.

It was only five kilometres to Maxine's and yet it felt like twenty. Time slipped away, our focus purely on seeing that headlight and then creeping forward. Every time we saw that headlight, we felt relieved. If the lead bike failed there would be no headlight to signal us, and it would be extremely difficult for our designated leader to make his way back to us.

Drum by drum we proceeded, the howling wind all but precluding communication even with the person next to you except by yelling at the top of one's lungs. It was better to conserve heat, keep our traps shut and use primitive sign language instead.

At last, we heard the prearranged signal that we were almost at the hut, the leader sounding the quad bike's horn, the honking sound blown to us on the wind. There, just ahead, revealed between gusts of spindrift was the green of the hut, a very welcome sight indeed.

On arrival at the hut we secured the bikes in a line to prevent too much drift covering them and beating the snow off our clothing, tumbled gratefully into the hut. At last, sanctuary! With the heater on and a hot cuppa in hand we chatted excitedly and a little hysterically about our journey, often talking all at once. Still high on adrenalin, we were aware of a lucky escape.

As the adrenalin wore off, we calmed down, the blizzard raging on outside. Dinner revived us and we discussed the event more rationally, the need to be more aware of wind direction and more importantly not to allow panic to overwhelm one's mind in a blizzard, or indeed in any potentially life-threatening situation. It was a lesson well learned.

Every night in the field there is a scheduled radio connection with station and the weather forecast is read out as part of the program. None of us had heard mention of a weather system coming although as we discovered it wasn't unheard of for minor systems to remain un-forecasted. We were glad to report that we were all safe and never mentioned our near miss.

In bed I listened to the howling gale, the blizzard now married to the katabatic, the winds were 50-knots gusting above 70, and even though heavily secured to the rock the hut shook under those mighty gusts.

Our recent adventure involved 35-knot winds, perhaps gusting to 50, and I felt extremely glad not to be out in the current conditions.

Morning came and the hut no longer shook. The blizzard had blown through and the katabatic was on the wane. By 10 am after a leisurely breakfast there was only a breeze and soon after, that too had ceased. The cloud had also passed, and we were back to blue skies. The rapidly changeable Antarctic weather had surprised us, but we had come though unscathed. We were due back on station for dinner so had the day to ourselves. A unanimous decision was made to remain local and just enjoy our surroundings which included a beautiful refrozen melt lake that was perfect for ice skating.

First, we excavated the quad bikes that were partly covered in snow drift. Every hut has a couple of snow shovels, so in ten minutes they were free. Then we started the bikes and ran them for a while to ensure that they were okay and in good running order for later.

Maxine's has several pairs of ice skates and while not always a perfect fit, an extra pair of socks tended to do the trick. The lake's surface was like polished glass, the frozen water so pure that the rocky bottom was visible about 15 feet below. There were strings of pearl like bubbles from near the bottom all the

Figure 104: A tentative ice skater busting some moves on the frozen lake at Rumdoodle.

215

way to just under the surface as well as ivory fault lines and spider web air pockets, that made the dark ice look like ancient marble.

None of us were experts at ice skating although one bloke was quite good. After an unsteady start, gaining balance and confidence, I glided in circles over the natural ice rink. In time, confidence growing I managed some figure of eights. Then, as is often the case, I became over-confident and tried some trickier manoeuvres which landed me on my ass, that later blossomed into a large multi-coloured bruise. I put it down to watching too much Olympic ice skating and returned to more manageable techniques.

We had great fun. Just imagine ice skating on the Antarctic icecap under blue sunny skies, incredible, immaculate, fantastic!

After lunch we lazed on the hut's deck sometimes dozing in the sun. Every now and then one of us would put the kettle on and fetch hot drinks and a packet of biscuits. Slowly we emerged from our stupor. I walked southwards around the rocky flank of Rumdoodle and past a wide-open valley to an easily climbed ridge. In the all-pervading silence I sat and looked to the south and was humbled once again by the enormity of Antarctica.

All packed up, we headed for station, taking our time, reluctant to return. We had climbed Mount Rumdoodle, gazed out over the icecap from the ridge leading to Fang Peak in the David Range, survived an unexpected blizzard and ice skated on the Antarctic plateau, all things that were beyond our imagining and that we would always remember.

Figure 105: A pause before descending to station. The image shows how steeply the plateau rises up directly behind the station, an elevation of around one-hundred-and-fifty-metres in about three kilometres. Bech is visible centre left.

CHAPTER 15:

BECH: LATE GUARD, CRÈCHE AND DEPARTURE

With the festive season over, it was great to be back on Bech with the penguins; I'd missed both them and our field camp home. They were now well into the second guard phase, and things were looking good. About 60 eggs had been lost during or after the incubation phase, due to a combination of reasons: infertility, abandonment, chilling following blizzards, eggs accidentally displaced from nests and/or losses to skuas. Over a dozen chicks had been taken by skuas during the early guard phase when they were light enough to snatch on the wing.

We carried out a count of the remaining chicks, the result incredibly positive; 1,819 chicks, ten chicks having been predated during our absence. Most of the active nests remaining had at least one chick, while many had two, the ratio about 60:40 in favour of single chick broods.

Chicks were being fed or lay sprawled, belly side down on the nest, sated from recent feeds. They were too large to be brooded although in harsh weather they thrust head and shoulders beneath their standing parent who leaned over them at about 45 degrees to gain some shelter themselves. Large fluffy bums stuck out from beneath the adult and if there were two chicks, there was shoving and wriggling, each

Figure 106: This shows the second part of the guard phase when the chicks are far too large to be brooded by the parent birds.

one attempting to gain the best protection from the cold. With rising temperatures, the katabatic wind was now not as cold, and blizzards were much less likely. In fine weather the chicks stood beside their guardian, avoiding the unwelcome attentions of aggressive neighbours.

The chicks looked like fat old men in slate grey jumpsuits, large pot bellies and rolls of fat at their chest and shoulders. Not quite as cute as the days following hatching but to compensate, they were developing real character. Pairs of chicks often pecked and barged each other to the point of jostling their long-suffering mum or dad. When the other adult returned from sea, the chicks joined their parents in bonding, whistling enthusiastically in time with the crowing of the adults. It would take several months for them to find their adult voice.

Pleasantries over, the chicks harassed the newcomer for food, who at first refused, a necessary action to encourage competition in two chick broods and/or to help stimulate regurgitation in the parent. But they were relentless in their demands, and while the other adult left for sea, its partner soon relented and fed the hungry chicks. Afterwards they were again sprawled on the nest, sated, dozing blissfully, at least until digestion led to further demands on their guardian.

In two chick broods it was often now obvious which had hatched first and got a head start on development, one chick visibly larger than the other. The single chicks were doing particularly well, the adults having long forgotten any lost offspring.

We were fully engaged in our twice daily nest monitoring and deploying the final batch of TDRs and satellite trackers. A few more birds were subjected to stomach flushing to assess what prey they were hunting and how much they were bringing back during this phase of chick development. As usual we

Figure 107: Chicks in single brood nests grow faster, as generally do the first chick to hatch in double brood nests.

took turns on surveillance duty, ready to spot birds returning with devices and then capturing them before they crossed the weighbridge and entered the rookery.

In the evenings I still found time to sit with the penguins, sometimes sketching them, especially the chicks. I'm no artist, this was purely for my own enjoyment. It made me look for the detail, the shape of the head and beak, the length of the flippers: their wonderful pot bellies. It was a peaceful time, the hubbub of the colonies receding into the background. I love the immediacy of wildlife, past and present are irrelevant to them; they invest everything in the moment. Disputes are quickly settled; they don't waste energy on resentment or worry. The business of feeding and rearing chicks was all that mattered. Due to their small and upright stature, their waddling walk and their curiosity, penguins are readily anthropomorphised: transformed into little people. Animated movies add to this, but it is no bad thing, penguins being one of the most beloved of animals on the planet. More love and interest in them may mean that people care more about their welfare and now with climate change threatening their very existence they need all the help they can get. Even with 3.8 million pairs of Adélie penguins around the Antarctic continent they are vulnerable to extinction due to their dependence on krill which in turn are dependent on the extent of the pack ice. Loss of pack ice would prove catastrophic for them and for emperor penguins too.

Up close and personal this wild bird species has tremendous presence. Ashore to breed –for a few of weeks of every year (their most important life event) we get to observe this vibrant creature that cannot be tamed. Penguins do not belong in zoos, my heart aches when I see them there (on TV I don't visit zoos) even though they are very well cared for. Concrete pools are no substitute for pack ice and open ocean.

Researchers are fortunate to witness their struggles, successes and failures during breeding. It is a humbling experience. They made me smile at their antics, yet I knew their purpose to be in great earnest and my respect and admiration for them grew every day that I was there. For a bird so perfectly adapted to a life underwater they get about on land extremely well. Their large feet and sharp claws provide good traction, and they can rock climb amazingly well.

We cannot follow them to sea, where they live for most of the year. When they depart the island following breeding, hopefully leaving one or two fledging chicks behind, they return to their true element, the ocean. I tried to follow them in my mind. Nobody really knows where they go, satellite trackers currently do not have the battery life to cover such a long period. But out there somewhere there are millions of Adélie Penguins, diving and hunting and then resting up on icebergs and icefloes through the Antarctic twilight and night. All to ensure that they are in good condition for another season, to do it all over again. Part of me would like to know where they go but another part prefers that it remains a mystery. Some things should, I think.

Meanwhile on Bech the Adélie penguin parents sense when the chick or chicks reach a certain weight, somewhere between 1.0 and 1.5 kilograms, and now require more food in order to grow faster and heavier. It coincided with the youngster(s) being able to thermoregulate, now having a layer of fat to maintain warmth in most weather conditions. To achieve the fledging weight both adults must now shuttle food from the ocean to the chick(s), so their offspring must be left unattended. It is a trade-off between the need for twice as much food and the potential for loss of chicks to skuas. But there is a solution to the problem.

Ten days after our return – we had made one last return trip to station – the first parent birds departed over the fast ice for sea, to join their mates, leaving their offspring unguarded. Other adults were still guarding their young, and unattended chicks were often harassed by them. To avoid this aggression the chicks were forced to make their way to open ground away from the colony and together with others formed aggregations or crèches of between a dozen and 30-40 individuals.

The crèches are also crucial in the defence against attack by skuas, unless of course a chick became isolated, skuas always being on the lookout for such opportunities. Even if this occurred the pair of skuas had their work cut-out, the chick now too heavy to drag away. Such attacks often failed, the chick stumbling back to the safety of the crèche, injured but alive to recover. A third benefit of crèches is that during harsh weather (and this is much less prevalent in summer) the chicks huddle together for warmth and thus conserve much needed energy.

Figure 108: Chick crèches with some youngsters lying stretched out on the ground to cool off. The photo was taken after the break-out of the fast ice which has yet to occur in the narrative.

Being mid-January with temperatures either close or above zero, the chicks cooled off by lying on their fronts in loose groups, legs and flippers outstretched. Blood vessels in their legs dilate to aid in cooling. They looked so peaceful lying there, such abandon in their demeanour, eyes closed, dozing in the sun. To the unknowing eye they appeared dead but should a skua come calling they were on their feet and clustered together in a flash.

Higher temperatures also meant that we could wear fewer layers of clothing while working, making us less encumbered. Early in the season we had to wear freezer suits beneath our outer work gear but now I wore only thin thermals beneath the heavy (and smelly) outer jacket and pants.

Now when a parent bird returned from the hunt, they had to separate their offspring from the others, there being many hungry chicks that might steal a meal. Once the chick or chicks awakened and identified their mum or dad, a chase ensued. The adult turned and ran, pursued by between one and six hungry chicks falling over themselves in their eagerness for food. The chicks looked like obese old men with a medicine-ball sized gut, running with flippers outstretched and legs spread to accommodate their bellies, sometimes falling on their faces then springing back up to continue the chase. The non-related chicks soon fell away, and if a single chick remained the chase might be over in 10 to 20 metres. Chases with two chicks were longer, perhaps 30 to 50 metres, sometimes 100, weaving and turning, often back towards the crèche. The fastest chick was usually fed first, but then with food in its belly it was slower on the next sprint and the second chick was fed. The chicks were now being fed every day or twice every three days and as a result grew faster.

Figure 109: The battle for food. Following a chase over the rocks the parent bird finally relents and feeds the chicks. The largest and usually the taller (normally the first to hatch) wins and the smaller one gets fed next.

We counted the chicks in the crèches: 1,809, a few having been taken by skuas during the late guard phase. This was one of the better years on Bech, in fact it was up there with the best since the study began in the late eighties. It felt great to know that so many chicks had survived and that when they left the island, they had a good chance at life.

I sat and watched the adults coming and going over the ice, that delicious waddle that every child knows thanks to so many penguin movies, animated or otherwise. With rapidly growing chicks I knew that the parade of adults would not last that much longer and I had to get my fill.

There were melt pools close to shore now and the adults took full advantage of their presence, having a good bathe before leaving the island and when returning after their long walk over the ice. The scene was always one of exuberance, it often made me smile, the thrashing and splashing, turning on one side and then the other, cleaning every part of their bodies after the filth of the rookery. The word 'relished' certainly applies to bathing penguins. This was always followed by a thorough preening, using oil from a glad near their tail to re-waterproof their feathers. There was also slushy snow on offer – as mentioned previously penguins (and other polar seabirds) eat snow to hydrate – and many adult Adélies were availing themselves of the bounty.

The fast ice was now cratered with pools of melt water that had refrozen overnight. Following our last trip to station the fast ice was closed to all travel, and we were now marooned on Bech until the ice broke out. It probably would not be long and could occur anytime between the third week of January and the beginning of February.

One night I sat on the northern shore of Bech several hundred metres from camp. The sun was now setting again, and the sky had that post-sunset misty, pastel shaded hue, a dreamy colour-blended sky of peach, pink and burnt orange. A moon, two thirds full, the

Figure 110: A lone Adélie penguin crossing fast ice cratered by summer-time refrozen melt pools. One of my favourite icebergs is top right. The image was taken soon after moonrise.

colour of red Leicester cheese rose over the ice, just to the left of my favourite icebergs, that were now firmly off limits. Way out on the ice that now looked like the cratered surface of the moon, between me and the icebergs, a lone penguin waddled by. It stopped and looked towards me, and a subtle exchange took place. I snapped a photo which although not clearly focussed takes me right back there to that incredibly peaceful, private moment between me and a solitary penguin under the orange moon. Then it waddled onwards and out of my line of sight. I sat there for another hour until a chilly breeze signalled the onset of the katabatic wind, just me and the liberating silence.

I thought about our trip earlier in the season to the Rookery Islands, an area of special scientific interest due to the presence of several species of breeding seabird including a colony of southern giant petrels. The area lies 10 kilometres to the west of Bech and is about 10 kilometres long and five kilometres wide with 30 or so islands and many clusters of rocks. The southern portion was dominated by loosely grouped block-of-flats sized icebergs with shimmering ice-ballrooms in between. It was another sight that I had never seen, palaces of ice in a frozen wonderland. I recalled standing there amongst it all, feeling like I was in a crystalline dream world and wondering how I could describe it to my friends.

Meanwhile, as the crèche phase progressed, the number of visits from the parent birds declined and then stopped, the chicks now at their maximum weight of roughly three kilograms. The adults were now free to remain at sea, preparing for the annual moult, an energy demanding process especially as Adélies, like other penguin species, replace all their feathers at once, a process known as a catastrophic moult. During this time, about two weeks or more, they do not enter the water, but stand around looking miserable, moulting an entire suit of feathers being a very itchy and uncomfortable affair. They don't necessarily return to Bech to moult, any island or stable iceberg will do.

Figure 111: An Adélie chick in the process of fledging. It looks messy but soon it will look just like its parent, apart from a white chin that will become black during the following years moult.

Once feeding ends, the chicks take a week or so to fledge. The white breast feathers appear through the dark fluffy down like a painting by a great master, covered for years by another, inferior painting and then slowly cleaned to reveal the original. Black feathers become visible on their backs at the same time, but many chicks are left with a pair of fluffy grey pantaloons, mink-like stoles around their shoulders and Mohican hairdos. The state of partial fledging looks comical but, in a few days, the ungainly juvenile would take to the sea and discover that it was born to live and hunt in the ocean.

They lose roughly 15% of their body weight – about 450 grams - between the end of feeding and when they are fully fledged, so on fledging they weigh only 2.5 kilograms. Hunger becomes the imperative for taking their first swim and going to sea, which with the ice gone would be right on their doorstep. I hoped to see some of them leave but we did not have a lot of time left, our own departure was drawing close.

But I am getting ahead of myself, the chicks have only just begun fledging and the fast ice still stretches to the horizon.

We went to bed on January 21st, the fast ice cratered and rotten, grey in places due to the dark ocean showing through. Overnight a storm blew in which coincided with a high tide and in the morning the ice was gone. A complete transformation had occurred, a vast plain of ice replaced by open jade-green water to the horizon but for the grounded icebergs, the wind whipping at the waves; white caps and blown spray.

I felt somewhat bereft. Even though ice travel had been over for two weeks, the fast ice still represented freedom. It had been my close companion for months and now so suddenly it was gone. It took a while to sink in, the shores now sea lapped, shallow bays of green water instead of thick ice. From Bech's summit looking south, waves broke at the base of the ice cliffs. That too took some mental adjustment.

Figure 112: Overnight the fast ice that had stretched to the horizon was gone. My icebergs were still there, although I could no longer get to them.

The upside to the break-out was that adult Adélie penguins feeding chicks now had no fast ice to cross in order to reach the sea, making their hunting forays even shorter. It also meant that when the fledgelings departed Bech, they would do so directly into the sea.

The wind blew all that day, preventing the boats from coming, but the day after the wind had died and we received a message via radio that they were on their way. This was not yet our final departure, a brief visit to station only. It felt strange boarding boats. There were always two for safety reasons; a zodiac-like inflatable and a much longer and more robust steel and fibreglass work boat with an open cabin.

On our return to Bech there were few adult penguins left and the island had grown mostly silent apart from the whistles of the chicks. We only had 10 days left on Bech. The *Aurora Australis* was due to arrive at Mawson on February 10th to resupply the station and to deliver the new winter crew as well as picking up current winterers and the summer personnel.

We cleaned all the equipment before stowing it either in the store shed or in the office pod, which was also thoroughly cleaned. We did an inventory of remaining food so that the resupply of Bech, conducted during winter, would be with the right quantities, and range of items. We took pride in cleaning every nook and cranny of the living pod; there was always thought for the next people to inhabit a space in Antarctica, as Bech would be used as a station get-away once the ice reformed in April and became thick enough for vehicular travel.

The day before we left, with most of our packing done, I had ample time for a final tour of the island and to conduct my last observations

Figure 113: Saying goodbye and farewell to the Bech snow petrels whose nests I had visited off and on daily for months. They seem so delicate and yet can be very feisty!

of the snow petrels. As usual in that endeavour I followed the western shoreline to a long upward sloping gully where some of the study nests were located. That took me onto broad fissured rock slabs beside which the overhangs provided nest cervices for the birds who were either still incubating an egg or brooding a recently hatched chick. I caught glimpses of tiny fluffy white chicks: an adult always present and keeping a close eye on me. As I sat nearby and wrote in my field book, I wished each one of the chicks success on their first flight and a long productive life.

I sat on the summit for an hour, snow petrels in the air all around me, briefly alighting on the rock slabs nearby. The scene before me and all around was so different now, although I had become used to it over the last nine days. Even so, the sight of the ocean everywhere that once was ice, including in Horseshoe Harbour was discombobulating.

I used the dumbbells one last time and once recovered from my exertions I said farewell to the snow petrels and dropped down off the ridge to Bech's southern shore. I walked the same route as though I was returning from staring into the blizzard's icy vortex, each boulder an ally. My last port of call was to my old friend turtle rock. I would miss our one-sided chats. I sat astride his or her neck (I could never decide on its gender) and thought back on my time on Bech and at Mawson. So many glorious events and sights, so many firsts, so many experiences that I would find nowhere else. The silence, ah the silence, it was so special in our over-populated world, so all encompassing; I hoped that it would remain with me, just within reach.

Next day the boats arrived to pick us up for the last time. I had already said my goodbyes to the fledging chicks, wishing them well on their life adventure. Our large bright red packs were already down by the landing area as we waited for the boats.

Figure 114: The boats arrive to pick us up from Bech for the last time.

A small group of Adélie chicks, earlier to fledge than the others, approached the shore as we sat there, and I found myself holding my breath. Would they go to sea: would we see it happen? They seemed to know that there might be monsters waiting for them, leopard seals now able to wait just offshore. I saw one or two nearby but with several other Adélie penguin colonies in the vicinity their visits were intermittent. I had encountered one hauled out on the ice earlier in the season and it had gaped a threat at me. With jaws bigger than a tiger and able to open them almost 180-degrees, they are fearsome things. They are wily hunters, so I understood perfectly the penguin's hesitation, nobody wants to go first, and it is better that all go at once to confuse the predator.

They moved closer to the water, jostling one another, hunger driving them on yet still wanting another bird to take the plunge first. Just as the boats came into sight one bird hopped to the water's edge, put

233

its head down and took the plunge, the others quickly following in a flurry of splashing. They swam away from the shore and surfaced further out as though to check that they had indeed left their grubby and ungainly land-based early life. Submerging again they disappeared, and it was as though they had recently come ashore and were now leaving again, instead of taking the first swim of their lives. I felt a surge of emotion; partly because I had hoped so much for this moment before we left but also because there was no sign of leopard seals, and the youngsters were safe. It was a precious moment, for my boss and I, the circle was closed, from egg to chick and now the first young birds had gone to sea.

My geologist friends had come out on the boats too which I felt grateful for, my sadness at leaving the birds and Bech eased by their friendly smiling faces. Once onboard the boat we did not return to station immediately but instead motored around the islands. A few

Figure 115: My friends having fun on a floating icefloe. I just missed photographing them as they played leapfrog. I love the contrasting colours of this image.

ice floes had been blown back in from sea and we laughed as the three geologists landed on one of them and proceeded to play leapfrog. Three colourfully dressed people on an alabaster ice floe surrounded by endless green water and a pearl-grey sky, it was a wonderful sight.

Having retrieved the three of them, the boats turned and retraced the route that the Hägglunds had taken so many months previously, when bringing us to Bech, through the narrow strait near Stinear Island. The big iceberg was still there, lapped now by wavelets, shining brightly in the sunlight. Crossing Kista Strait we arrived at the landing site just below the station to a warm welcome from a small group of our friends.

CHAPTER 16:

RESUPPLY AND DEPARTURE

Three days after leaving Bech the *Aurora Australis* appeared out to sea and navigating the islands and channels of Holme Bay, pulled into Horseshoe Harbour, its bright orange raiment complementing the primary colours of the station buildings. Moored fore and aft on both sides within a hundred metres of West Arm, the 95-metre vessel dominated the harbour. It felt strange to see her again, having spent six weeks on board on my way to Mawson. Instead of the *Aurora* being stuck with a damaged rudder 400-kilometres away in the pack ice all those months ago, she was now able with the fast ice gone, to steam straight into the harbour.

Figure 116: The Aurora Australis lit up by the setting sun, moored in an ice-free Horseshoe Harbour with the Flat Islands beyond.

With hundreds if not thousands of kilometres of open water instead of extensive pack ice, her arrival time had been predicted to the hour and the station personnel were ready and waiting. A large crane was deployed near the landing point, the goods brought ashore in steel pallets, mainly by two flat barges, offloaded by a 20-tonne crane and then moved to wherever they were required by eleven tonne front-end loaders. Two squirrel helicopters would also be doing short trips to carry slung loads to shore. In this way 370-tonnes of goods would be transferred from ship to shore and driven directly to the massive forest green store shed where crews of helpers would unpack and stow them. Enough food and other consumables for another year would come ashore as well as dozens of 200-litre barrels of special Antarctic blend unleaded petrol for quad bikes and generators as well as barrels of aviation fuel for refuelling helicopters.

As ever, the first items to come ashore were fresh fruit and vegetables, the fruit fallen upon by the expeditioners as though by marooned sailors, the first fresh produce in several months. Next came the mail packages containing goodies not available on station. Once the stores and other goods were offloaded, a special crew went to work rolling out and testing fuel hoses that would pump 800,000-litres of special Antarctic blend diesel into the massive fuel tanks near the shore. The row of black tanks, as big as road fuel tankers, were protected by a surrounding concrete basin in case of fuel spillage although hose and valve testing carried out in Hobart and on station meant that spills were highly unlikely.

The ship's arrival had been eagerly anticipated especially by the outgoing winter crew who had been away from home for a year, some of them longer. Personnel, like myself, who had been there for spring and summer were also going home and the new winter crew of 18 deployed.

The four-day ship visit was also the handing over period between the outgoing and incoming crews, the new station leader being shown all the relevant tasks and issues regarding running the station while the trades and scientific staff did the same in their respective areas.

I had been moved to an outside hut or donga, an insulated container that was comfortable enough. My meals and hot showers were still in the red shed. With so many people on station the outgoing chef and his incoming colleague were kept busy, the usual slushy (or kitchen helper) roster being doubled. Meals were in two sittings during the ship's stay.

Several rosters had been posted on the stations information board and we had been given a briefing by both the station leader and voyage leader regarding duties but especially safety issues around the helicopter marshalling area and the large front-end loaders operating between the shore and the store shed. I had a couple of slots as slushy as well as spells in the main store helping to unpack pallets of goods and then stack them away. During resupply nobody was permitted to travel outside of station limits without the station leader's permission.

The weather, generally good at this time of year, held and resupply went well. The Katabatic was less fierce but still precluded work after 10 pm and before 10 am which suited many of us very well. Twelve hours of work is enough for anyone, although most of it was done by heavy lift vehicles.

I learned that many years later, with the ship moored in the same place as always, a severe blizzard had hit, and the mooring lines had been put under enormous pressure. A shackle had snapped, and the other three mooring lines also parted, leading to the ship running aground on West Arm, in the process holing a ballast tank. Fortunately, the hole could be patched, and the vessel re-floated and so was able to continue her voyage. But henceforth the resupply vessel was anchored outside of the harbour and kept underway in blizzard conditions to avoid running aground.

In the evenings after work, I wandered within station limits and on one occasion a friend and I walked up towards the plateau, breaking the rules a little but not by too much. The view back over the station and the Big Orange Ship in the harbour was magnificent, beyond lay the islands, Bech prominent amongst them. The sun was setting, and all was bathed in golden light, the open water to the horizon broken only by the odd iceberg, my two favourite bergs still in place, no doubt to be frozen in again when the fast ice reformed in mid-to-late March.

On the last evening, with the ship due to depart next day, I walked out on West Arm and up to the three crosses that mark the graves

Figure 117: An Adélie penguin emissary come to say goodbye to me (in my mind at least!), with the jumble of colours of the ship and station behind. One of the three memorial crosses is visible.

of men who died at Mawson, one during a tobogganing accident, the second from perforated ulcers and septicaemia and the third as a result of a fall on the ice while dog sledding. All incredibly sad events that rocked the small station crews of the 1963, 1972 and 1974 winter seasons. I stood for a moment in remembrance and when I looked up there stood a single Adélie penguin. It cheered me to see it. It was as though one of their kind had been sent as an emissary to say a last farewell and I chatted to it amiably for a while.

Next evening, we said our farewells and on boarding the ship we found our allocated cabins. Many of us had single occupancy cabins which was fantastic, quite different to my outward journey.

In gentle twilight, the ship got underway, at first manoeuvring carefully through 180-degrees to point in the right direction and then slowly steaming out of the harbour. The remaining winterers clustered on shore at the end of West Arm to see us off while those on board lined the port side rail. As was tradition at Mawson, out-of-date flares were ignited by those on shore, the small crowd wreathed in red and orange smoke, the flares looking like handheld roman candles.

There were three mighty blasts from the ships horn as we passed through the harbour heads while shouted farewells flew back and forth from ship to shore and back again. The coloured smoke swirled and eddied, blending to form a drifting magenta cloud, the figures amongst it spectral and appearing a little forlorn. They would not see any other people now for over seven months.

Once we were beyond the islands, the orange pods of Bech field camp now out of sight, people drifted below. I stood at the stern rail and said a silent thank you to Antarctica for my time there and to its magnificent wildlife, neither of which I would ever forget.

Figure 118: The traditional send off from Mawson. The folk onshore are staying throughout the coming winter and won't see another soul for several months.

With open ocean and very little pack ice we would be at Davis in two days with a further 10-days across the wild Southern Ocean back to Hobart. Once we were far enough north, darkness would once again claim the nights and we would see stars and perhaps the southern lights for the first time in months.

As we steamed away from Mawson, even the vast continent was lost to sight in the twilight, only the odd iceberg breaking the ocean vista. I popped a couple of seasickness pills and with a last look back towards the frozen continent, headed below for dinner.

EPILOGUE

The *RSV Aurora Australis* recently entered retirement after 30 years of excellent service to the Australian Antarctic Division and to ANARE. She was replaced by a much larger, purpose-built research and resupply vessel (red in colour) that can break ice up to 1.65 metres thick. The iconic orange ship will be missed by many, but her name lives on, the new vessel, named *RSV Nuyina*, is Tasmanian aboriginal for the southern lights or aurora australis.

Awareness of human induced climate change has grown in our psyches from the early concerns of climate scientists into an impending crisis and now an emergency. The polar regions are warming much faster than the rest of the planet. Increased ice melt in the Arctic and collapsing ice shelves in West Antarctica herald a frightening new era. The human population, whether it knows it or not, is in trouble and is facing an unstable climate that will trigger increasingly extreme climatic events. The world's wildlife has no knowledge of our crazy human ways and yet tens of thousands of species may pay the highest price: extinction.

This book is a celebration of Antarctica and of the unique wildlife that lives and breeds there. I hope with every fibre of my being (as I'm sure you do too) that they continue to do so, sending future generations into a world where they not only survive but thrive. It is up to all of us, and especially large corporations and our elected governments, to act decisively now.

On a personal note, I never returned to Antarctica although years later I travelled twice more on the *Aurora Australis*, this time to sub-Antarctic Macquarie Island where I worked as a ranger (1999) and then later as a site inspector for the Australian Bureau of Meteorology (2009 and 2012). My journey to Antarctica and my time at Mawson remain some of my most treasured life events.

REQUEST TO READERS

If you enjoyed this book, and even if you didn't, can you please take the time to review it on Amazon and other platforms, as it would help me very much. I don't get out much these days and don't have influential friends or publishers to review the book for me. In any case I prefer my readers to do so.

A percentage of any proceeds I receive from the sale of this book will be donated to either Cancer Research UK or Cancer Care in my local area of West Cumbria, UK.

My very best wishes,
Michael Anderson.
birdsbeastsandice@gmail.com

ACKNOWLEDGEMENTS

I owe a great debt of gratitude to Susan Sheriden, my friend and unpaid volunteer editor. I can never repay your kindness and expertise. Thank you! I will endeavour to be better at grammar, to learn to breath and to use apostrophe's correctly!

To my wife Jane whose support of my writing means the world to me.

To the Australian Antarctic Division without whom I would not have set foot in Antarctica.

I am greatly indebted to the Australian scientific research community, past and present, for information on Adélie penguins, emperor penguins, snow petrels, Weddell seals and Antarctic krill. Other disciplines that contributed to my understanding of Antarctica include geology and meteorology as well as studies of sea ice, glaciology and the marine environment.

ABOUT THE AUTHOR

Michael and his wife Jane both retired in 2017 and moved from a bush property in southern Tasmania to a houseboat on an estuary in West Cumbria, UK. They live in a post-industrial landscape that has evolved into fascinating wild spaces and it is this recovery of nature that inspires them. Being only twenty minutes from the Lake District National Park Jane and Michael have many wonderful opportunities to enjoy varied landscapes and wildlife.

In June 2019 Michael was diagnosed with advanced prostate cancer and he and Jane have been doing their utmost to remain positive. Michael can no longer walk very far but his beautiful wife and the natural world sustain him. He does not reveal his condition for sympathy reasons, living with cancer is just a fact of life. He does so because he feels that awareness of this and other cancers is essential. Cancer research and new treatments give people hope and it is that which sustains Michael and Jane. He says that 'we need to continue to encourage governments to fund such programs including Cancer Care, a not-for-profit organisation that has helped Jane and I a great deal.'

Michael's love of wildlife began when he was five years old and living in southern Scotland. He had the run of a nearby deciduous woodland and a small river (or burn) to himself. It was there that he learnt to be still and to open his senses. Once the wildlife, especially the birds, settled to his presence he could observe them and learn about their behaviour. This simple pleasure has been with him ever since.

Michael says that 'sitting quietly with breeding Adélie and emperor penguins, snow petrels and Weddell seals was quite literally out of this world, and he wanted to share his experiences in this book. He says, 'I hope very much that you enjoyed it and that you love Antarctica and its wildlife as much as I do.'

Above are a few of the sketches that Michael did while sitting near the Adélie penguin chicks in their crèches on Bech.

Lightning Source UK Ltd.
Milton Keynes UK
UKHW020840151022
410462UK00002B/4